Resurrection and Easter Faith

Lenten Bible Study and Discipleship Lessons

Bible Study Commentary for Personal Devotional Use, Small Groups or Sunday School Classes, and Sermon Preparation for Pastors and Teachers

JesusWalk® Bible Study Series
by Dr. Ralph F. Wilson
Director, Joyful Heart Renewal Ministries

Additional books, and reprint licenses are available at:
www.jesuswalk.com/books/resurrection.htm

Free Participant Guide handout sheets are available at:
www.jesuswalk.com/resurrection/resurrection-lesson-handouts.pdf

JesusWalk® Publications
Loomis, California

Paperback
    ISBN-13: 978-0-9847340-1-6
    ISBN-10: 0984734015

Library of Congress Control Number: 2011918833

Library of Congress subject heading:
        Jesus Christ - Resurrection.

Suggested Classifications
        Dewey Decimal System: 232.5
        Library of Congress: BT481

Published by JesusWalk® Publications, P.O. Box 565, Loomis, CA 95650-0565, USA.

JesusWalk is a registered trademark and Joyful Heart is a trademark of Joyful Heart Renewal Ministries.

Unless otherwise noted, all the Bible verses quoted are from the New International Version (International Bible Society, 1973, 1978), used by permission.

111017

Preface

It seems like the bodily resurrection of Jesus Christ from the dead is always under attack from one quarter or another.

In March 2007, Titanic director James Cameron made news by promoting a documentary claiming the discovery of The Lost Tomb of Jesus,[1] purporting to contain the ossuaries of Jesus' family – Jesus, Mary Magdalene, and their child Judah. Besides being based on bogus research and shoddy scholarship, it is an insult to Christians who know there aren't any bones to be found. Christ is risen!

But unfortunately this kind of attack isn't confined to non-Christians. Retired Episcopalian Bishop John Shelby Spong reduces the disciples' proclamation of the resurrection of Christ to a way of saying that

Matthias Grünwald (German painter, c. 1480-1528), "Resurrection" (1512-1516), 106x112.5 in., right interior panel of the Isenheim Altarpiece (Diptych), Unterlinden Museum, Colmar, Alsace, France.

> "... In the particular life of the spirit person Jesus, they saw not only God, but also a picture of what each of us might look like in our fulfilled spirit state."[2]

---

[1] "The Lost Tomb of Jesus" (VisionTV, 2007). www.jesusfamilytomb.com.
[2] John Shelby Spong, *Why Christianity Must Change or Die* (HarperSanFrancisco, 1998), pp. 115-117.

German theologian Rudolf Bultmann ascribed the accounts of the resurrection to subjective visions that Jesus' disciples experienced.[3] Professor Gerd Lüdemann wrote that Jesus' body may be rotting in the ground, but to the question, Can we still be Christians? one can answer a confident Yes.[4]

The truth about the resurrection matters. If Jesus wasn't raised bodily from the dead then Christianity is a sham, a pious fraud, a failure. Paul wrote some twenty centuries ago:

> "And if Christ has not been raised, your faith is futile; you are still in your sins. Then those also who have fallen asleep in Christ are lost. If only for this life we have hope in Christ, we are to be pitied more than all men." (1 Corinthians 15:17-19)

Our study begins with the assumption that the Bible accounts should be taken seriously. We don't reject resurrection out of hand because it requires a belief in miracles. Instead, we seek to understand what the scriptures actually say about the subject.

First, we examine resurrection from its earliest mentions in the Old Testament to Jesus' teaching about resurrection. Then we look at the accounts in each of the four gospels to determine to the best of our ability exactly what took place that Easter morning. Next, we survey alternate explanations of the resurrection and discuss the strong facts of the resurrection that underlie our belief in Christ's physical resurrection from the dead. Then we explore the theological and practical implications of Christ's resurrection. Finally, we consider what the New Testament teaches about our own resurrection on the Last Day.

I've included the URLs to each of the discussion questions in this book so, if you like, you can read others answers and post your own thoughts about the questions.

---

[3] Rudolf Bultmann, *Kerygma and Myth* (SPCK, 1953), pp. 38-42, cited by Paul Beasley-Murray, *The Message of the Resurrection* (Inter-Varsity Press, 2000), p. 242.

[4] Gerd Luedemann, *The Resurrection of Jesus: History, Experience, Theology* (translated by John Bowden; Fortress Press, 1994), p. 180-183.

My prayer is that as you study about the resurrection your knowledge will be increased, your faith grounded solidly in the Word of God, and your hope polished to see ahead the return of Christ and your own resurrection at the Last Day.

Dr. Ralph F. Wilson
Wildwood, Loomis, California
Lent 2007

Table of Contents

Reprint Guidelines

Copying the Handouts. In some cases, small groups or Sunday school classes would like to use these notes to study this material. That's great. An appendix provides copies of handouts designed for classes and small groups. There is no charge whatsoever to print out as many copies of the handouts as you need for participants.

All charts and notes are copyrighted and must bear the line: Copyright © 2011, Ralph F. Wilson. All rights reserved. Reprinted by permission.

You may not resell these notes to other groups or individuals outside your congregation. You may, however, charge people in your group enough to cover your copying costs.

www.jesuswalk.com/resurrection/resurrection-lesson-handouts.pdf

Copying the book (or the majority of it) in your congregation or group, you are requested to purchase a reprint license for each book. A Reprint License, $2.50 for each copy is available for purchase at

www.jesuswalk.com/books/resurrection.htm

Or you may send a check to:

Dr. Ralph F. Wilson
JesusWalk Publications
PO Box 565
Loomis, CA 95650, USA

The Scripture says,

> The laborer is worthy of his hire (Luke 10:7) and Anyone who
> receives instruction in the word must share all good things with
> his instructor (Galatians 6:6).

However, if you are from a third world country or an area where
it is difficult to transmit money, please make a small contribution
instead to help the poor in your community.

References and Abbreviations

BDAG   Walter Bauer and Frederick William Danker, *A Greek-English Lexicon of the New Testament and Other Early Christian Literature* by (Third Edition; based on a previous English edition by W.F. Arndt, F.W. Gingrich, and F.W. Danker; University of Chicago Press, 1957, 1979, 2000)

DJG   Joel B. Green, Scot McKnight, and I. Howard Marshall (editors), *Dictionary of Jesus and the Gospels*, (InterVarsity Press, 1992)

DLNT   Ralph P. Martin and Peter H. Davids (editors), *Dictionary of the Later New Testament*, edited by (InterVarsity Press, 1997)

Grudem   Wayne Grudem, *Systematic Theology: An Introduction to Biblical Doctrine* (Inter-Varsity Press/Zondervan, 1994, 2000)

ISBE   Geoffrey W. Bromiley (general editor), *The International Standard Bible Encyclopedia* (Eerdmans, 1979-1988; fully revised from the 1915 edition)

KJV   King James Version (1611)

Ladd   George Eldon Ladd, *I Believe in the Resurrection of Jesus* (Eerdmans, 1975)

McDowell Josh McDowell, *Evidence that Demands a Verdict* (Campus Crusade for Christ, 1972)

NRSV   *New Revised Standard Version* (Division of Christian

Education, National Council of Churches of Christ in
the USA, 1989)

NIV   *New International Version* (International Bible Society,
               1973, 1978, 1983)

TDNT   Gerhard Kittel and Gerhard Friedrich (editors),
               Geoffrey W. Bromiley (translator and editor),
               Theological Dictionary of the New Testament (Eerd-
               mans, 1964-1976; translated from *Theologisches
               Wörterbuch zum Neuen Testament*, ten volume edition)

Wright   N.T. Wright, *The Resurrection of the Son of God*
               (Fortress Press, 2003)

1. The Promise of Resurrection from the Dead

I would guess that many Christians today believe more in the immortality of the soul than in resurrection. A belief in going to heaven is much more in mind than one's body being physically raised from the dead. But resurrection from the dead – especially Jesus' own bodily resurrection from the dead after his crucifixion – is the centerpiece of Christianity.

Fra Angelico (c. 1400-55), Resurrection of Christ and Women at the Tomb (1440-41), Fresco, 189 x 164 cm, Convento di San Marco, Florence

In this five-week series were going to examine resurrection carefully. Well begin by looking its Old Testament roots, Jesus' teaching on the subject, and Jesus' own resurrection from the dead. Then well explore the meaning and significance for us of Jesus' resurrection, as well as the proofs we have that his resurrection actually took place. Finally, well consider what the Bible says about the resurrection of our own bodies.

Resurrection Defined

Let's begin by defining some terms. By life after death people are usually referring to the state of being alive, conscious, or something, after the physical phenomenon of death. But by resurrection we are referring not just to the soul or spirit, but specifically to the physical body in some way. The Greek word for resurrection (*anastasis*), comes from the verb *anistēmi*, to raise, arise. The other verb used occasionally is *egeirō*, to awaken, rise. Not that the Greeks believed in resurrection. They didn't. The New Testament uses these words to describe a raising up of the body after a period of being dead. The New Testament teaches a raising of our physical bodies at the Last Day to even more life than they had when we were alive before.

Gathered to their Father's

But such a belief wasn't always the case. When we turn back to the era of the Old Testament, in the earliest days, we don't see a belief in resurrection. In Genesis, for example, when Abraham died, he was gathered to his fathers (Genesis 25:8). This probably meant that his bones would be stored with theirs, referring to the ancient and widespread practice of secondary burials, collecting and storing the bones after the flesh has decomposed.[1]

Sheol, the Shades

In the earlier part of the Old Testament we also find the Hebrew word *sheôl*, the place of the dead, both good and bad. While the KJV often translates it as hell, more recent translations render it the grave (NIV) or the realm of the death, or just leave it untranslated and render it as Sheol[2] (NRSV). Sheol seems to refer to the dark, deep regions, the land of forgetfulness ... a place of gloom and despair, a place where one can no longer enjoy life, and where the presence of Yahweh himself is withdrawn.[3] Thus we find in the Psalms:

> "No one remembers you when he is dead.
> Who praises you from the grave (*sheôl*)?" (Psalm 6:5)

---

[1] Wright, *Resurrection,* pp. 90-91.
[2] R. Laird Harris, *shāal,* TWOT #2303c.
[3] Wright, pp. 88-89.

> "Do you show your wonders to the dead?
> Do those who are dead rise up and praise you?
> Is your love declared in the grave,[4]
> your faithfulness in Destruction?[5]
> Are your wonders known in the place of darkness,
> or your righteous deeds in the land of oblivion?"
> (Psalm 88:10-12)

The First Glimmers in Job

But gradually, slowly, God begins to reveal to his prophets that there is something more than darkness beyond death. Theologians call this revealing of more truth as time goes on, progressive revelation. Job wonders:

> "If a man dies, will he live again? All the days of my hard service I will wait for my renewal to come." (Job 14:14)

Later he declares with longing:

> "I know that my Redeemer lives,
> and that in the end he will stand upon the earth.
> And after my skin has been destroyed,
> yet in my flesh I will see God;
> I myself will see him
> with my own eyes — I, and not another.
> How my heart yearns within me!" (Job 19:25-27)

This passage is notoriously difficult to translate.[6] But is Job beginning to see something beyond the grave? I think so.

Q1. How does Jobs vision of resurrection (Job 19:25-27) differ from the Jews former understanding of death as Sheol? What is progressive revelation?
http://www.joyfulheart.com/forums/index.php?showtopic=567

---

[4] Hebrew *qeber*, "grave, sepulcher" (R. Laird Harris, *qābar*, TWOT #1984a).
[5] Hebrew *ăbaddôn*, "destruction, ruin, Abaddon," from *ābad*, "perish, be destroyed," a common word for "to die" (R. Laird Harris, *ābad*, TWOT #2d).
[6] Wright, *Resurrection*, pp. 97-98.

Psalm 16 Refers to Resurrection

A Psalmist declares:

"Therefore my heart is glad and my tongue rejoices;
my body also will rest secure,
because you will not abandon me to the grave (*sheôl*),
nor will you let your Holy One see decay.
You have made known to me the path of life;
you will fill me with joy in your presence,
with eternal pleasures at your right hand." (Psalm 16:9-11)

Resurrection in Hosea

In the Prophet Hosea we read:

"I will ransom them from the power of the grave (*sheôl*);
I will redeem them from death.
Where, O death, are your plagues?
Where, O grave, is your destruction?" (Hosea 13:14)[7]

In Hosea 6, we see an intriguing passage, apparently interpreted in terms of resurrection by Jesus himself:

"Come, let us return to the LORD;
for it is he who has torn, and he will heal us;
he has struck down, and he will bind us up.
After two days he will revive us;
on the third day he will raise us up,
that we may live before him." (Hosea 6:1-2)[7]

It is the first passage that seems to make the explicit statement that Yahweh will give his people a new bodily life on the other side of death.[8]

---

[7] Wright (*Resurrection*, p. 118) asserts that the original Hebrew text is almost certainly denying that YHWH will redeem Israel from Sheol and Death. However, the LXX and other ancient versions, and also the New Testament, take the passage in a positive sense.

[8] Wright, *Resurrection*, p. 119.

The Resurrection in Isaiah

Isaiah the Prophet speaks even more clearly of a bodily resurrection:

"But your dead will live;
their bodies will rise.
You who dwell in the dust,
wake up and shout for joy.
Your dew is like the dew of the morning;
the earth will give birth to her dead." (Isaiah 26:19)

At the conclusion of the Suffering Servant passage of Isaiah 53, we see a wonderful glimmer of hope, brought out best by the New International Version:

"After the suffering of his soul,
he will see the light of life and be satisfied;
by his knowledge my righteous servant will justify many,
and he will bear their iniquities." (Isaiah 53:11)

The phrase light of life (NIV) doesn't occur in the Masoretic Hebrew text, but is found in both the Greek Septuagint translation as well as the Hebrew text of the Isaiah scroll found among the Dead Sea Scrolls.[9] The Servant's contemporaries saw him as cut off from the land of the living (53:8). But 53:11 indicates that the Servant will see light – that is, life outside the grave – even after his atoning death. I expect that Jesus also saw this promise, which underlies his teaching to his disciples that it is written that the Son

---

[9] This verse can be construed in various ways. The Masoretic Text, which underlies the KJV, does not include the Hebrew noun *or*, "light" (NRSV) or "light of life" (NIV). However, they appear in the both the Septuagint and in all the Dead Sea Scroll (Qumran) copies of Isaiah, which constitutes strong evidence (John N. Oswalt, *The Book of Isaiah: Chapters 40-66* (New International Commentary on the Old Testament; Eerdmans, 1998), p. 399, fn. 43. Light can symbolize general life (Herbert Wolf, TWOT #52). On Psalm 36:10, Mitchell Dahood (*Psalms* (Anchor Bible; Doubleday) 1:221-222) argues that to see light is often really to see the light of God's face in immortality, though this may refer to mortal life as perhaps Psalm 49:19 (so Peter C. Craigie, *Psalms 1-50* (Word Biblical Commentary, vol. 19; Word, 1983), p. 292) See a similar idea in Psalm 17:15.

of Man would be raised from the dead (Luke 24:25-27; 8:31; 9:31; 10:32-34; 14:21).

The Valley of Dry Bones in Ezekiel

In Ezekiel we see a kind of resurrection:

> "I saw a great many bones on the floor of the valley, bones that were very dry.
> He asked me, Son of man, can these bones live?
> I said, O Sovereign LORD, you alone know.
> Then he said to me, Prophesy to these bones and say to them, Dry bones, hear the word of the LORD! This is what the Sovereign LORD says to these bones: I will make breath enter you, and you will come to life. I will attach tendons to you and make flesh come upon you and cover you with skin; I will put breath in you, and you will come to life. Then you will know that I am the LORD." (Ezekiel 37:2b-6)

This may not be an actual prophecy of resurrection as much as a figure of the restoration of a nation. Nevertheless, it added to the Israelites consciousness of resurrection.

Daniel 12:1-2

Probably the clearest reference in the Old Testament to resurrection is found in Daniel:

> "There will be a time of distress such as has not happened from the beginning of nations until then. But at that time your people – everyone whose name is found written in the book – will be delivered. Multitudes who sleep in the dust of the earth will awake: some to everlasting life, others to shame and everlasting contempt." (Daniel 12:1b-2)

First Century Judaism

By the time the first century rolled around, resurrection – which had just a few references in the Old Testament – was now held by the largest number of people in Judaism. There were essentially three beliefs about the resurrection in Jesus' world.

Sadducees

The Sadducees represented the aristocrats, a minority group that held a good deal of power in Judaism. They held a considerable number of seats on the Sanhedrin, the ruling council. The high priests families were also Sadducees (Acts 5:17). They denied the resurrection of the dead on the last day, and held to a view that the dead were in Sheol, as some of the earlier portions of the Old Testament had taught. They didn't take this position because they were the liberals; rather they were the conservatives of the time. Since the resurrection wasn't clearly mentioned in the Pentateuch (the first five books of the Bible) and the historical books, they refused to accept it (Matthew 22:23; Acts 23:8). However, the Sadducees didn't exist as a major group in Judaism after the destruction of Jerusalem in 70 AD.

Pharisees

The Pharisees strongly held the view that the there was a resurrection. They were a reform party in Judaism, who believed in a serious commitment to holiness and obedience to every command in the Bible. However, their reformation had become hardened into a brittle and self-serving personal righteousness that tended to keep the letter of the law, but often missed the spirit of the command. Some of Jesus' most scathing commentaries on contemporary Judaism were directed at the Pharisees – though he agreed with them about the resurrection of the saints at the Last Day.

The Greeks and Romans

The third major group was represented by the Greco-Roman beliefs held by the Roman governor and the army of occupation. They weren't Jews, of course, but represented the dominant worldview met by the apostles when they began to preach the resurrection of Christ outside of Israel in the Mediterranean world. Greeks believed in the immortality of the soul, but scorned the resurrection of the body as a silly belief (Acts 17:18, 32).

Previous Resurrections

There had been restora-
tions to life before in the
history of Israel. Elijah had
restored the son of the
widow of Zarepheth (1
Kings 17:17-21). Elisha had
raised the son of the
Shunnamite woman (2
Kings 4:32-35). Jesus had
raised Jairus' daughter
(Mark 5:40-42) and the son
of the widow of Nain (Luke
7:11-15). Of course, Jesus'

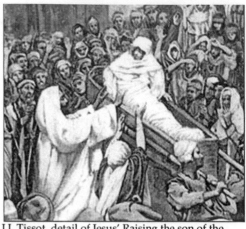
J.J. Tissot, detail of Jesus' Raising the son of the widow at Nain (1890), original watercolor.

friend Lazarus was raised after having been dead four days (John
11). At the hour of Jesus' death, Matthew records that the bodies
of many holy people were raised to life (Matthew 27:51-53). These
resurrections are treated as harbingers of Jesus' coming resurrection, proof that Jesus had death in his own control.[10] The
difference between these resurrections and the resurrection of
Jesus and the saints on the Last Day was that these people later
died.

Jesus' Teaching on the Resurrection of the Dead

Now, let's examine what Jesus himself taught about the resurrection from the dead. He affirmed that:

> "Those who have done good will rise to live, and those who
> have done evil will rise to be condemned." (John 5:28-29)

Jesus' statement echoed Daniels prophecy and paralleled the
Pharisees teaching of a resurrection of both the righteous and the
wicked. (Acts 24:15). Jesus taught that this would be a time of

---

[10] Grant R. Osborne, "Resurrection," DJG 673-688.

reward for those who had followed the Lord: You will be repaid at the resurrection of the righteous (Luke 14:14).

Q2. (John 5:28-29; Acts 24:15) According to scripture, both the righteous and unrighteous will experience resurrection. What will be the result of resurrection for the righteous?
http://www.joyfulheart.com/forums/index.php?showtopic=568

When the Sadducees asked Jesus a trick question to try to poke fun at the resurrection, Jesus told us something about state of believers at the resurrection:

The people of this age marry and are given in marriage. But those who are considered worthy of taking part in that age and in the resurrection from the dead will neither marry nor be given in marriage, and they can no longer die; for they are like the angels. They are God's children, since they are children of the resurrection. (Luke 20:34-36)

On that occasion, Jesus also taught that the resurrection of the dead is implied even in the Pentateuch that the Sadducees claimed to honor above all other scriptures:

But in the account of the bush, even Moses showed that the dead rise, for he calls the Lord the God of Abraham, and the God of Isaac, and the God of Jacob. He is not the God of the dead, but of the living, for to him all are alive. (Luke 20:37-38)

Jesus' as the Agent of Resurrection

For Jesus, however, the resurrection wasn't just a belief about a future event. He would be intricately involved himself as the Agent of Resurrection. At the time of Lazarus death, the following exchange took place between Jesus and Lazarus sister Martha:

"Jesus said to her, 'Your brother will rise again.'
Martha answered, 'I know he will rise again in the resurrection at the last day.'

Jesus said to her, 'I am the resurrection and the life. He who believes in me will live, even though he dies; and whoever lives and believes in me will never die.'" (John 11:23-25)

Another place, Jesus said:

"I tell you the truth, a time is coming and has now come when the dead will hear the voice of the Son of God and those who hear will live.... A time is coming when all who are in their graves will hear his voice and come out – those who have done good will rise to live, and those who have done evil will rise to be condemned." (John 5:25, 28-29)

In the discourse about bread, Jesus asserted that he himself would raise up his disciples on that day:

"And this is the will of him who sent me, that I shall lose none of all that he has given me, but raise them up at the last day. For my Father's will is that everyone who looks to the Son and believes in him shall have eternal life, and I will raise him up at the last day.... Whoever eats my flesh and drinks my blood has eternal life, and I will raise him up at the last day." (John 6:39-40, 54)

Q3. (John 11:23-25) What do you think Jesus meant when he said, I am the resurrection and the life? What role will Jesus play in the resurrection of the dead?

http://www.joyfulheart.com/forums/index.php?showtopic=569

Jesus' Promise of His Own Resurrection

Even more striking is Jesus' teaching that he himself would be raised from the dead on the third day. Jesus predicts both his death and resurrection three times during the latter part of his ministry:

"From that time on Jesus began to explain to his disciples that he must go to Jerusalem and suffer many things at the hands of the elders, chief priests and teachers of the law, and that he must be killed and **on the third day be raised to life."** (Matthew 16:21; cf. Luke 9:22)

"When they came together in Galilee, he said to them, 'The Son of Man is going to be betrayed into the hands of men. They will kill him, and **on the third day he will be raised to life.'"** (Matthew 17:22-23)

"Now as Jesus was going up to Jerusalem, he took the twelve disciples aside and said to them, 'We are going up to Jerusalem, and the Son of Man will be betrayed to the chief priests and the teachers of the law. They will condemn him to death and will turn him over to the Gentiles to be mocked and flogged and crucified. **On the third day he will be raised to life!'"** (Matthew 20:17-19; cf. Luke 18:31-33)

The Third Day, Three Days

Jesus used two figures to speak elliptically of his resurrection on the third day. First, the figure of the temple:

"Then the Jews demanded of him, 'What miraculous sign can you show us to prove your authority to do all this?'
Jesus answered them, 'Destroy this temple, and I will raise it again in three days.'
The Jews replied, 'It has taken forty-six years to build this temple, and you are going to raise it in three days?' But the temple he had spoken of was his body. After he was raised from the dead, his disciples recalled what he had said. Then they believed the Scripture and the words that Jesus had spoken."
(John 2:18-22)

Jesus' enemies remembered this saying at his trial (Matthew 27:40; Mark 14:58). The second figure Jesus used was the story of Jonahs three days in the fish's belly as a sign of his own resurrection (Matthew 12:39-40). Though it didn't really seem to register with his disciples (Luke 24:7-8), his words weren't lost on the Pharisees and chief priests:

"The next day, the one after Preparation Day, the chief priests and the Pharisees went to Pilate. Sir, they said, we remember that while he was still alive that deceiver said, After three days I will rise again. So give the order for the tomb to be made secure until the third day. Otherwise, his disciples may come and steal the body and tell the people that he has been raised from the dead. This last deception will be worse than the first.'" (Matthew 27:62-64)

And so Pilate ordered a guard to be placed. We make a distinction between three days and the third day, but in Greek, these two phrases meant the same.[11] After his resurrection, Jesus explained: "This is what is written: The Christ will suffer and rise from the dead on the third day...." – probably a reference to both Hosea 6:1 and Isaiah 53:11.

Q4. Why did Jesus' enemies heed his prediction of being raised on the third day even more than his disciples? Did his enemies expect him to rise? Did his followers?
http://www.joyfulheart.com/forums/index.php?showtopic=570

The resurrection of the dead was the strong expectation and hope of Jesus. Is yours? In the next lesson we will examine Jesus' own resurrection from the dead.

Prayer

Lord, implant in us the strong faith in the resurrection that Jesus himself held. In Jesus' name, we pray. Amen.

Key Verses

"I know that my Redeemer lives,
and that in the end he will stand upon the earth.
And after my skin has been destroyed,
yet in my flesh I will see God;

---

[11] Ladd (*Resurrection*, p. 109) writes: "Students of the Greek language have proven that, contrary to English usage, the two phrases were identical in meaning." He cites for this Vincent Taylor, *The Gospel according to St. Mark* (London: Macmillan, 1952), p. 378.

I myself will see him
with my own eyes – I, and not another.
How my heart yearns within me!" (Job 19:25-27)

"There will be a time of distress such as has not happened from the beginning of nations until then. But at that time your people – everyone whose name is found written in the book – will be delivered. Multitudes who sleep in the dust of the earth will awake: some to everlasting life, others to shame and everlasting contempt." (Daniel 12:1b-2)

"Jesus said to her, 'I am the resurrection and the life. He who believes in me will live, even though he dies; and whoever lives and believes in me will never die.'" (John 11:25-26)

2. The Gospel Accounts of Christ's Resurrection from the Dead

Note: Before beginning, read the Resurrection accounts in the Gospels. Try looking at them as for the first time. Ask yourself: What happened here that prompted these stories? Look for differences as well as similarities.

- *Matthew 28:1-10*
- *Mark 16:1-14*
- *Luke 24:1-44*
- *John 20:1-29*

If you like, refer to the parallel accounts in Appendix 1.

El Greco (Spanish painter, 1541-1614), "The Resurrection" (1596-1600), Oil on canvas, 275 x 127 cm, Museo del Prado, Madrid.

When we come to the four accounts of Jesus' own resurrection, we see strong similarities plus a number of mainly minor differences. How reliable are the Gospel accounts of the resurrection? What do they tell us about what really happened? How are we to understand the differences? Is there a clear resurrection message?

The Synoptic Problem

Even a casual reader will notice that the first three gospels – Matthew, Mark, and Luke – have many verbal similarities, while the fourth gospel seems quite different. Because they have so much common material, the first three gospels are termed the Synoptic Gospels. The word synoptic comes from two Greek words *syn-*, "together" + *opsesthai*, "to see." It means presenting or taking the same or common view.

Scholars have hypothesized, rightly, I believe, that the writers of the Synoptic Gospels must have had some common source document available to them that contained the stories and teachings of Jesus, some kind of proto-gospel. Scholars have a name for this hypothetical source; they call it Q, which stands for the German word *Quelle*, meaning source.

The gospel writers, I assume, probably drew on Q and wove it together with their own eyewitness material and other traditions to fashion an account of Jesus' life and teachings for their particular audience. Obviously, each gospel writer told the story with a particular editorial purpose in mind. Mark's gospel is commonly agreed to be the earliest gospel. Matthew's gospel seems to be written especially with Palestinian Jews in mind, and takes special care to point out Jesus' words and actions as the fulfillment of Old Testament prophecies. Luke's gospel seems to speak to a Hellenistic audience. The Gospel of John, on the other hand, didn't seem to use this Q source at all. As an eyewitness, John wrote from his own mature perspective of what Jesus said and did and intended.

When you compare the gospels, you see some minor differences here and there. That's just the way the Gospels have been given to the Church. We may not understand the reasons for these differences; we just accept them and let the scholars spin their complex theories.

Resurrection Differences

The gospel accounts are similar, but each is different. Let's look at them carefully.

First of all, it's pretty clear that Mark 16:9-19, the so-called longer ending of Mark, wasn't part of the original gospel, that ended – at least the surviving edition that we have – with verse 8. Perhaps the last page was lost. Verses 9-19 were added by the early church because it seemed strange that Mark ended abruptly as it did. Not that these verses are misleading, but they aren't part of the original gospel.

When you compare each of the stories, you can find a number of differences. For example:

1. *Women.* In the Synoptic Gospels, Mary Magdalene and other women go to the tomb. In Johns account, Mary Magdalene goes alone.

2. *Appearance to the women.* In Matthew 28:9, Jesus appears to the women before they tell the disciples. In John 20:13-17, Jesus appears to Mary Magdalene (also in the longer ending of Mark) – *after* she reports to the disciples. In Mark, the women tell no one of what they had seen.

3. *Number of angels.* In Matthew and Mark one angel appears; in Luke and John there are two angels.

4. *Purpose of the women's visit.* In Matthew, they go to look at the tomb. In Mark and Luke, they bring spices to anoint Jesus' body. In John the anointing took place on Friday night and no purpose for Mary's visit is given.

5. *Grave clothes.* In Matthew and Mark, Jesus is wrapped in a large linen shroud (*sidrōn*). In John 19:40; 20:5-7 and Luke 24:12, Jesus is wrapped in strips of linen (*othonion*). See the discussion below.

6. *Location.* In Matthew and Mark, Jesus' resurrection appearances are in Galilee, while Luke only records appearances in the vicinity of Jerusalem.[1]

My point isn't to try to pick apart the account or cause you to disbelieve it. But to stimulate you to see what's there. Most of these differences are minor and can be explained or harmonized rather easily.[1]

---

[1] This section draws heavily on Ladd, *Resurrection*, pp. 84-88.

Eyewitness Accounts

A more troubling question is if eyewitnesses can't seem to get their stories straight, whether we can believe the story or not. When you think about it, you realize that these very differences validate the authenticity of the story.

Whenever you have eyewitnesses testify to any event that they all see, there'll be minor points of difference in what they saw and how they perceived the event. If all the eyewitnesses agree in every detail, a good investigator begins to suspect collusion between the witnesses before testifying.

The Church has been aware of these minor differences in the resurrection accounts for many centuries. Some might express concern with how this might affect our doctrine of the authority of scripture (2 Timothy 3:16). But surely our understanding of the inspiration of scripture must be large enough to encompass the gospel accounts as we find them. Rather than seeing these accounts as evidence of error, the Church has viewed them as evidence of authenticity, representing various eyewitness traditions that are remarkably united on the main points.

Q1. What differences do you find between the various resurrection accounts? How do you account for differences in eyewitness testimony? How might these differences add to the credibility of the witnesses?
http://www.joyfulheart.com/forums/index.php?showtopic=571

Points of Agreement

In the big, important things we see five main points of agreement. They include:

1. Jesus was dead and buried.
2. The disciples were not prepared for Jesus' death. They were overcome with confusion.

3. The tomb was found on Easter morning to be empty. But this in itself didn't inspire faith. Mary thought the body was stolen.

4. The disciples encountered a number of experiences that they took to be appearances of Jesus risen from the dead.

5. The disciples proclaimed the resurrection of Jesus in Jerusalem, near where he had been buried.[2]

What Happened Easter Morning?

It is possible to so analyze the event that we miss the big picture: That Jesus who was dead had been raised from the dead.

- Mary Magdalene saw him first and spoke to him (Mark 16:9, longer ending; John 20:16)

- Other women also saw him and touched him (Matthew 28:9).

- Jesus appeared to Peter and the other apostles (Luke 24:34; 1 Corinthians 15:5; Mark 16:14 longer ending; Luke 24:36).

- Jesus appeared to Thomas (John 20:26-28).

- Later, Jesus appeared to more than 500 people at one time (1 Corinthians 15:6).

The disciples who were in deep depression after his crucifixion were finally convinced that he had indeed risen from the dead. That is what happened on Easter morning. That amazing fact is underscored in each of the gospels. Paul summed it up this way:

"For what I received I passed on to you as of first importance: that Christ died for our sins according to the Scriptures, that he was buried, that he was raised on the third day according to the Scriptures, and that he appeared to Peter, and then to the Twelve. After that, he appeared to more than five hundred of the brothers at the same time, most of whom are still living, though some have fallen asleep. Then he appeared to James,

[2] Ladd, *Resurrection*, pp. 93.

then to all the apostles, and last of all he appeared to me also...."
(1 Corinthians 15:3-8)

Q2. What similarities do you find in the resurrection accounts? Based on the agreements between the accounts, what seems to have happened?
http://www.joyfulheart.com/forums/index.php?showtopic=572

The Grave Clothes

All the accounts credit Joseph of Arimathea with wrapping Jesus' body in a linen cloth (*sindōn*) or linen cloth wrapping (*othonion*). Two words are used here for the grave wrappings.

Strips of linen (NIV) or linen clothes (KJV) is *othonion*, (linen) cloth, cloth wrapping. There is some debate between the translation of strips of linen (NIV) or larger cloth wrappings.[3]

---

[3] *Othonion*, BDAG 693. The term *keiria*, "binding material," used to describe Lazarus grave wrappings, may refer to some kind of webbing (BDAG 538). C.K. Barrett (*The Gospel According to St. John* (Second Edition; Westminster Press, 1978), p. 404) sees the meaning bandage attested in the papyri, and observes that such winding strips that seem to have been in use in Jewish practice. He sees *othonion* as a linen bandage, such as might be used for wrapping a corpse (*John*, p. 559), and cites Moulton and Milligan for the phrase *othonia euona*, "fine linen wrappings for a mummy." Catholic scholar Raymond E. Brown (*The Gospel According to John* (Anchor Bible; Doubleday, 1970), 2:941-942) provides an extended note designed to defend the idea that the Shroud of Turin (a linen sheet 14 feet long and 4 feet wide) could have been described by *othonia*, rather than the modern interpretation of linen strips or bandages. He says there is no evidence that Jews wrapped their corpses with bands or strips similar to those used for Egyptian mummies. Granted the obscurity of the term, he concludes, we had best translate it vaguely as cloth wrappings. Danker observes concerning the word *othonion*, "The applicability of the sense bandage in our literature is questionable" (BDAG 693).

Fine linen (KJV) or linen cloth (NRSV, NIV) is *sindōn*, presumably a large piece of linen in which the body was carried from the cross to the tomb, and then wrapped around him.

Eugène Burnand (French painter, 1850-1921) "The Disciples Peter and John Running to the Sepulcher on the Morning of the Resurrection" (1898), Paris, Musée d'Orsay.

Though some see a conflict between strips of cloth and a large linen cloth, I don't see any. When you compare Luke 23:53 (*sindōn*) with Luke 24:12 (*othonion*) it appears that Luke, at least, is using the terms synonymously.

The position of the grave clothes in the tomb attracted the apostles attention and caused Peter and John to believe:

> "Peter, however, got up and ran to the tomb. Bending over, he saw the strips of linen (*othonion*) lying by themselves, and he went away, wondering to himself what had happened." (Luke 24:12)

> "[The other disciple] bent down to look in and saw the linen wrappings (*othonion*) lying there, but he did not go in. Then Simon Peter, who was behind him, arrived and went into the tomb. He saw the strips of linen (*othonion*) lying there, as well as the burial cloth (*soudarion*) that had been around Jesus head. The cloth was folded up by itself, separate from the linen (*othonion*). Finally the other disciple, who had reached the tomb first, also went inside. He saw and believed." (John 20:6-8)

The napkin (KJV) or burial cloth (NIV) that had been on Jesus' head was folded separately. Ladd says that this was a separate piece of cloth that was wrapped over the head and under the chin to prevent the jaw from sagging.[4]

What was so startling? That the linen was lying there neatly.

1. If Jesus' body had been stolen, grave robbers wouldn't have taken the time to unwind the shroud. In fact, the shroud would have helped them carry the body more easily.
2. If Jesus had been in a coma and revived, somehow he would have had to unwind the grave shroud in order to walk free.

The presence of the grave clothes neatly folded on the shelf were mute testimony that Jesus' body had slipped free of the grave clothes without disturbing them whatsoever. It was not the empty tomb that convinced the apostles. As Michael Perry puts it,

"It seems to be the evangelists intention to suggest that Peter saw the grave clothes like a chrysalis out of which the risen body of the Lord had emerged."[5]

The grave clothes didn't need to be unwrapped to let Jesus out, he passed from the grave clothes while they were still rolled up around his body.

Q3. (Luke 24:12; John 20:6-8) What about the grave clothes brought Peter and John to faith? What was so peculiar about them?
http://www.joyfulheart.com/forums/index.php?showtopic=573

Why Was the Stone Rolled Away?

Matthew's account tells us:

---

[4] Ladd, *Resurrection*, p. 94.
[5] S.H. Hooke, *The Resurrection of Christ* (London: Darton, Longman and Todd, 1967), p. 79, cited by Ladd, *Resurrection*, p. 94.

"There was a violent earthquake, for an angel of the Lord came down from heaven and, going to the tomb, rolled back the stone and sat on it. His appearance was like lightning, and his clothes were white as snow. The guards were so afraid of him that they shook and became like dead men." (Matthew 28:2-4)

The account may have come down to us through one of the soldiers, for by the time the women arrived, the stone had already been rolled back. Have you ever asked *why* the stone was rolled away?

The stone wasn't rolled away to let Jesus out of the tomb. If his body could pass through grave clothes and locked doors, escaping the tomb wouldn't have been any problem, rather, the stone was rolled away as a sign of God's power to the soldiers, to draw the disciples' attention to the empty tomb, and to let humans in to see.

What Was Jesus' Body Like?

Was Jesus raised bodily from the dead? That is, was his resurrection body the same physical body as before? The answer is yes, but more.

The gospels give us several characteristics of Jesus' resurrection body:

- Jesus described it as flesh and bones (Luke 24:39c).
- He could eat (Luke 24:42-43; Acts 1:4).
- His body could be touched and handled by others (Matthew 28:9; Luke 24:39b).
- He could walk and talk (Luke 24:15), even cook (John 21:9), just as a normal human body.
- Yet Jesus' wounds were still visible in his renewed body (Luke 24:39-40; John 20:20, 25-27).
- Jesus could be recognized by others – but only when he wanted to be. The timber of his voice remained the same (Matthew 28:9; Luke 24:16, 31; John 20:14-16, 20; 21:4, 12).

- Jesus could enter locked doors (John 20:19, 26) disappear (Luke 24:31) and appear (Luke 24:36) at will.

What I see in Jesus, is that his resurrection body had the ability to navigate in the physical world, but was not limited to the physical plane. In lesson 5, we'll talk more about what *our own* resurrection bodies will be like.

It is clear that the New Testament intends us to see Jesus' resurrection body not as something completely different than his physical body. It is clearly one that has continuity with the old, but it includes new powers and abilities.

Was Jesus raised bodily from the dead? The clear testimony of the Gospels is: Yes, indeed!

Q4. What do we know from the Gospels about the properties of Jesus' resurrection body? What was he capable of in this new body?
http://www.joyfulheart.com/forums/index.php?showtopic=574

The Resurrection vs. the Ascension

Before we leave the Gospels, it is important to make one distinction that is sometimes blurred in trying to understand the resurrection, that Jesus' resurrection and his ascension are two related but different events.

1. **Jesus' resurrection** was when his body left the tomb and appeared alive to his disciples and others, never to die again.

2. **Jesus' ascension** occurred about 40 days after his resurrection and took place just outside of Jerusalem near Bethany:

   "After the Lord Jesus had spoken to them, he was taken up into heaven and he sat at the right hand of God." (Mark 16:19, longer ending)

   "When he had led them out to the vicinity of Bethany, he lifted up his hands and blessed them. While he was blessing them, he left them and was taken up into heaven. Then they worshiped him and returned to Jerusalem with great joy." (Luke 24:50-52)

"I wrote about all that Jesus began to do and to teach until the day he was taken up to heaven.... After his suffering, he showed himself to these men and gave many convincing proofs that he was alive. He appeared to them over a period of forty days and spoke about the kingdom of God." (Acts 1:1-3)

"... After he said this, he was taken up before their very eyes, and a cloud hid him from their sight. They were looking intently up into the sky as he was going, when suddenly two men dressed in white stood beside them. Men of Galilee, they said, why do you stand here looking into the sky? This same Jesus, who has been taken from you into heaven, will come back in the same way you have seen him go into heaven." (Acts 1:9-11)

Jesus' resurrection refers specifically to his victory over death. His ascension to the right hand of the Father refers specifically to his exaltation by his Father to the highest place. Sometimes in the New Testament these are combined together as being glorified, exalted, or entering into his glory. Jesus' ascension is the final aspect of his resurrection from the dead; his ascension to his original and rightful place in God's presence.

Q5. What is the difference between Jesus' resurrection and his ascension? How do the two fit together? In what sense is the ascension the completion of the resurrection?
http://www.joyfulheart.com/forums/index.php?showtopic=575

The Bottom Line

The bottom line for Christians is this:

- Jesus predicted his death and resurrection on the third day.
- Jesus was raised bodily from the dead.

- Jesus ascended into heaven and sits at the right hand of God the Father.

The evidence that Jesus' resurrection actually took place is excellent, as well see in the next lesson. No other major religion claims the resurrection of its founder. And it makes a difference in what we believe will happen in the future.

Because Jesus lives, our hope in God is rock solid and our confidence in the future guaranteed!

Prayer

Father, thank you for Christ's willingness to endure the cross for the joy that was set before him. Thank you for the clarity with which the gospels tell us the good news of the resurrection. Help us to proclaim it unashamedly. In Jesus' name we pray. Amen.

Key Verses

"[The other disciple] bent down to look in and saw the linen wrappings lying there, but he did not go in. Then Simon Peter, who was behind him, arrived and went into the tomb. He saw the strips of linen lying there, as well as the burial cloth that had been around Jesus' head. The cloth was folded up by itself, separate from the linen. Finally the other disciple, who had reached the tomb first, also went inside. He saw and believed." (John 20:6-8)

"Mary Magdalene went to the disciples with the news: 'I have seen the Lord!' And she told them that he had said these things to her." (John 20:18)

3. Convincing Evidence of Christ's Bodily Resurrection

It doesn't surprise me that Christians need to convince agnostics and atheists, Buddhists, Hindus, Muslims, and Jews of the resurrection of Jesus Christ from the dead. But what astounds me is that by far the most learned and agile opponents of the physical resurrection of Jesus Christ are liberal Christian scholars. For example, here is the fairly accurate book description for *The Resurrection of Jesus*, by Gerd Lüdemann:

Giovanni Bellini (Venetian painter, c. 1430-1516) Resurrection of Christ (1475-79), Oil on panel, 148 x 128 cm, Staatliche Museen, Berlin.

> "What actually happened at the resurrection of Jesus? Using historical criticism and depth psychology, Lüdemann reviews the accounts of witnesses, consults Pauline texts, and investigates Easter events, concluding that *though the quickening of Christ cannot be believed in a literal and scientific sense, we can still be Christians.*"

People Just Don't Come Back to Life

The real issue is one of assumptions and worldview. Scholarly opponents of a literal, bodily resurrection assume a Western scientific worldview. If something cannot be explained or proved by science, then it is unscientific and false. There is no room whatsoever in this worldview for a God who intervenes in history, as does the God of the Old and New Testaments. There is only room for scientifically explained cause and effect within a closed system that excludes miracles. This is a determined unbelief in anything outside of a carefully defined worldview.

Liberal Christian scholars may assume that their sophisticated unbelief in the resurrection from the dead is new. It is not. As long as men and women have been alive on the earth they have experienced death and reflected upon it. They know that while people sometimes live a long time, they don't come back to life once dead.

The Epicurean and Stoic philosophers who heard Paul preach on Jesus' resurrection made fun of him (Acts 17:18, 32). Their worldview included the immortality of the soul, but not physical resurrection of the dead.

But for many people who are struggling with their own mortality, the news that Jesus overcame death and was raised to life gives them hope. Resurrection is actually Good News. In fact, the resurrection of Jesus is the core of the good news preached by the early church.

Historically Accessible

Liberal Christian scholars have retreated into a fuzzy but intellectually respectable agnosticism about what can be known from history. For example, Gerd Lüdemann, whose book was described above says:

> "We can no longer understand the resurrection of Jesus in a literal sense, i.e. in a bloody way ... for historically speaking we do not know the slightest thing about the tomb (was it empty? was it an individual tomb at all?) and about the fate of Jesus' corpse: did it decay? At any rate I regard this conclusion as unavoidable."[1]

---

[1] Gerd Lüdemann, *The Resurrection of Jesus: History, Experience, Theology* (translated by John Bowden; Fortress Press, 1994), p. 180. Lüdemann continues, "To the question: Can we still be Christians? the answer has to be a confident Yes.... The man Jesus is the objective power which is the enduring basis of the

With liberal Christian scholars, in addition to their intellectual pride, the primary hurdle to overcome is philosophical. To them, Jesus' resurrection can't be examined with the normal tools of historical inquiry because it is:

- **Unrepeatable.** It is a one-of-a-kind event that can't be studied.

- **Incomparable.** We have no analogies to which to compare it.

- **Lacks credible evidence.** This isn't actually true, but these scholars often explain away or neglect the strong evidence that we *do* have.

A Narrow View of Historicity

N.T. Wright, who strongly defends the resurrection, sees the idea of history used in five different ways in our modern culture:

1. History as an event. Something that happened, whether we can prove it or not.

2. History as significant event. An historic event is one which carries momentous consequences.

3. History as a provable event. X may have happened, but since we can't prove it, therefore it isn't really historical.

4. History as writing about events in the past. It is historical in the sense that it was written about – or talked about, as in oral history.

5. History as what modern historians can say about a topic, that which can be demonstrated and written within the post-Enlightenment world view. This is what liberal scholars mean when they reject the historical Jesus.[2]

I would argue that the resurrection is historical in senses 1, 2, 3, and 4. It cannot, however, be demonstrated and written about

---

experiences of a Christian.... We must stop at this historical Jesus, but we may believe that he is also with us as one who is alive now" (pp. 182, 183).

[2] Wright, *Resurrection*, pp. 12-13.

within the closed Western worldview that *a priori* rejects miracles. It is on these narrow grounds that liberal scholars claim not to know whether the resurrection took place or not. Mind you, it is not the common man that splits these historical hairs, but rather the liberal scholar who uses them as a dodge behind which to make unbelief seem respectable.

In fact, actual historians examine events that happened two or three millennia ago all the time. There *are* accepted ways to determine historical probabilities. The problem with the resurrection is not that it can't be demonstrated historically, but that it can't be explained in naturalistic terms. The explanation requires a recognition that God has intervened in history.

Alternate Theories of the Resurrection

Before we look at the strong historical proofs for the resurrection, let's consider the theories that one must adopt if he doesn't believe in the Biblical account that God raised Jesus from the dead bodily. I've looked hard to find and categorize the alternate theories floating around, which attempt to explain the disciples' belief in the resurrection. They come down to five theories, each with variations:

1. Theft theory
2. Swoon theory
3. Wrong tomb theory
4. Vision Theory
5. Spiritual Metaphor Theory

Let's briefly examine these one by one. After we do so, well examine in detail the five strong reasons why Jesus' bodily resurrection from the grave is the only adequate way to explain the data.

Q1. What do you think motivates liberal Christian scholars to explain away the bodily resurrection of Jesus Christ? Why would they claim that it is unhistorical more than some other event in the first century?
http://www.joyfulheart.com/forums/index.php?showtopic=576

1. Theft Theory

The theft theory is probably the first explanation given by Jesus' enemies and is still propounded by opponents of the resurrection today. When the soldiers reported to the chief priests that the stone had been rolled away, they were given a large sum of money to tell the story that His disciples came during the night and stole him away while we were asleep (Matthew 28:11-15)

The problems with this explanation are three-fold: (1) The disciples had no motive to steal the body. (2) Roman soldiers who fall asleep on watch are subject to death. (3) The disciples wouldn't have died for a faith they knew not to be true.

Some people have proposed that Jesus' enemies stole the body. But they had no motive either. They wanted Jesus well buried. If they had stolen the body, when the apostles began preaching the resurrection in Jerusalem, they could have ended Christianity's 15 minutes of fame by merely producing the body. They didn't. Why? Because they didn't have Jesus' body.

Q2. On the theft theory, what motive might the disciples have to take Jesus' body? What motive might the Romans have? The Jews? Joseph of Arimathea?
http://www.joyfulheart.com/forums/index.php?showtopic=577

2. Swoon Theory

According to the swoon theory, originally propounded by a German scholar Heinrich Paulus beginning in 1802, Jesus didn't really die, but weakened by loss of blood and his wounds, he slipped into a coma and was presumed dead. Later, in the cool of the tomb, he revives and leaves the tomb.

The problems in this theory are the spear thrust to his side, which apparently pierced his pericardium and released blood and water, signifying death. If Jesus had survived, the cool of the tomb would be more likely to kill than revive him. Moreover, in his weakened condition he would have to unwrap himself from the burial wrappings – or be helped by friends. But where's the motive?

A twist on this theory was propounded Hugh J. Schonfield (1901-1988), a British Biblical scholar, in his novel *The Passover Plot* (1965), later made into a movie (1976). The plot was that, with Jesus' collusion, Joseph of Arimathea was to drug him to make him unconscious and get him off the cross alive. This theory assumes that Jesus lived out the remainder of his days in hiding. But it isn't psychologically sound, as well see shortly.

3. Wrong Tomb Theory

The wrong tomb theory was developed by Kirsopp Lake (1872-1946), a noted English Biblical scholar and Harvard professor who wrote *Historical Evidence for the Resurrection of Jesus Christ* (1907). In it, he suggests that the women mistook the location of the actual tomb where Jesus' body lay. Instead, a young man, guessing their errand, points them in the right direction saying, He is not here, see the place where they laid him (misquoting Mark 16:6), but the women misunderstand, are frightened, and flee.[3] Later they

---

[3] Kirsopp Lake, *The Historical Evidence for the Resurrection of Jesus Christ* (New York: G.P. Putnams Sons, 1907), pp. 250-253, quoted by McDowell, *Evidence*, pp. 265-266.

mistakenly think the young man was announcing the resurrection.[4]

The problem, of course, is that Mary Magdalene had been to that tomb two days prior on Friday night (Matthew 27:61; Mark 15:47). In addition, it bore the seal of Rome and there was a guard of Roman soldiers camped in front of it. They couldn't have missed it. If this theory were true, all the Jewish authorities would have needed to do to refute claims of the resurrection would be to produce Jesus' body. They didn't.

4. Vision Theory

The vision theory was the fall-back position of one of the most influential opponents of the bodily resurrection in the twentieth century, German New Testament scholar Rudolf Bultmann (1884-1976). He sought to demythologize the gospel to make it believable to modern man. He wrote in 1941 of the incredibility of a mythical event like the resuscitation of a corpse – for that is what resurrection means.[5] Since a bodily resurrection was out of the question for Bultmann, he theorized that the disciples experienced subjective visions that convinced them that Jesus had risen from the dead. He wrote,

> "The historian can perhaps to some extent account for that faith [in the resurrection] from the personal intimacy which the disciples had enjoyed with Jesus during his earthly life and so reduce the resurrection appearances to a series of subjective visions."[6]

Later he seems to have retreated some from this position and declared that how the disciples' faith arose was not of basic

---

[4] As outlined by Ladd, *Resurrection*, p. 136.

[5] Rudolf Bultmann, *Kerygma and Myth* (SPCK, 1953), pp. 38-42, cited by Paul Beasley-Murray, *The Message of the Resurrection* (Inter-Varsity Press, 2000), p. 242.

[6] Bultmann, *Kerygma and Myth*, p. 42, cited by Ladd, *Resurrection*, pp. 136-137.

importance.[7] Johannes Weiss calls this "a profound inner conviction which, through an overwhelming final experience, emerges at last into certainty and reality."[8]

In other words, the disciples eventually come to believe that Jesus was resurrected because no other explanation of his death would do. It doesn't explain the exploding growth of the Jerusalem church based on the preaching of the resurrection. To refute this, all Jesus' enemies would have to do would be to produce the body. Sometimes called the Personality Influence Theory or the Hallucination Theory,[9] this is a desperate theory without support. It is inconsistent with the disciples' mental state and doesn't explain Jesus' appearance to 500 persons at once.

I'm almost embarrassed to mention Michael Perry's theory that Jesus communicated to his disciples by telepathy that he had truly conquered the powers of death.[10] It is novel, let us say, though it has no basis in the facts of the New Testament.

5. Spiritual Metaphor Theory

The spiritual metaphor theory is the final alternate theory of the resurrection, fairly common in our time among liberal pastors and theologians. It asserts that the disciples, especially Paul, didn't really believe in a bodily resurrection, but held a more spiritual view. Early Christians used terms such as dying and rising as a kind of metaphor to communicate their faith. When they said, Jesus was raised from the dead, so this view goes, they meant something like: He is alive in a spiritual, non-bodily sense,

---

[7] "How the Easter faith arose in individual disciples has been obscured in the tradition by legend and is not of basic importance." Rudolf Bultmann, *Theology of the New Testament* (New York: Scribners Sons, 1951), I. p. 45), cited by Ladd, p. 137.

[8] Johannes Weiss, *Earliest Christianity* (New York: Harper and Brothers, 1959), I, p. 30, cited by Ladd (p. 137).

[9] Thoroughly refuted by McDowell, *Evidences*, pp. 257-265.

[10] Outlined by Ladd, p. 139, citing Michael Perry, *The Easter Enigma* (London: Faber & Faber, 1959).

and we give him our allegiance as our lord.[11] Only later did the church begin to take such expressions literally, according to this theory, and then penned the gospel accounts as a kind of secondary reinforcement of this belief. This fuzzy-headed thinking doesn't understand Paul well, ignores the early date of the gospels, and bypasses the gospel accounts of the resurrection.[12]

In a nutshell, these are the five alternate theories that are supposedly more possible or historical than the gospel account itself. Instead, none of these alternate theories deals adequately with the historical material we have in front of us – the New Testament. Instead, they make unspoken assumptions and don't really add up.

Five Important Facts of Easter Morning

What does add up to a credible story, however, is the evidence of the New Testament. In Lesson 2, we examined various elements of the gospel accounts. Here let's examine the cumulative power of the account that makes it by far the most plausible explanation of what happened on Easter morning. These arguments can be summed up in five points.

1. The Empty Tomb
2. The Undisturbed Grave Clothes
3. The Disciples' Psychological State
4. The Post-Resurrection Appearances of Jesus
5. The Growth of Christianity

---

[11] Marcus J. Borg, in Marcus J. Borg and N.T. Wright, The *Meaning of Jesus* (London: SPCK, 1999), chapter 8, cited in Wright, *Resurrection*, p. 718. This general approach is discussed by Wright, *Resurrection*, pp. 7, 701-706.

[12] Of course, the New Testament does use dying and rising as analogies of the spiritual life (Romans 6:4-10; Colossians 2:12-13; 3:1; Ephesians 2:5-6; etc.). But that doesn't prove that they didn't really believe in a literal, bodily resurrection. The actual resurrection provides the basis and vocabulary for the analogy.

1. The Empty Tomb

The first important fact of Easter morning is that tomb is empty. This in and of itself didn't create faith in the resurrection. To Mary Magdalene it was a sign of grave robbers.

But any explanation of the resurrection must deal with the fact that Jesus' tomb was empty. In other words, there must be some explanation of what happened to his body. The theft, swoon, and wrong tomb theories above have rather lame explanations, though they deal with the issue. But the vision and spiritual metaphor theories essentially ignore the fact that Jesus' body isn't in the tomb. Any explanation of what happened Easter morning must deal with the fact that the tomb was empty.

2. The Undisturbed Grave Clothes

The second important fact of Easter morning is that two of the gospel accounts make it clear that Jesus' grave clothes lay essentially undisturbed on the stone shelf within the tomb. None of the alternate theories above even attempt an explanation.

If the grave clothes were missing or even thrown on the floor it could have meant that Jesus' body had been stolen or even revived and left. But for them to be still folded as they had been when they had been wrapped round and round Jesus' body is very strange. It indicates that his body just slipped out of them without disturbing them. The best explanation is that Jesus' body was raised from the dead miraculously by God. Any explanation of what happened on Easter morning must explain the position of the grave clothes.

3. The Disciples' Psychological State

The third important fact of Easter morning is the disciples' psychological state, which is mentioned in all four gospels. They were in hiding, discouraged, and disheartened. They did not at first believe the women's report of Jesus' resurrection. Only after Jesus appeared to them in person did they believe.

This indicates several things:

- That they weren't inclined to concoct a story of Jesus' resurrection.

- They weren't inclined to mistake Jesus' missing body for resurrection.

- They didn't expect any resurrection, even though Jesus had predicted it on at least three occasions. Jesus' crucifixion for them was an indication that their Messiah had been discredited.

- They weren't inclined to steal Jesus' body.

But let's suppose for a moment that they *were* part of a conspiracy to steal Jesus' body and claim that he had been raised from the dead. Of the original 12 disciples, ten were martyred for their faith. Only John seemed to have died of natural causes. As Origin put it, men do not risk their lives and suffer martyrdom for a lie.

To assume that the disciples were part of a conspiracy doesn't jive with a careful assessment of their psychological state. To suppose that the disciples of Jesus, the man of truth, would perpetrate a fraud is preposterous. When you consider the disciples' psychological state following Jesus' crucifixion, only the fact of the resurrection can explain the change that took place in them.

Q3. How does the disciples' psychological state after the crucifixion provide excellent support for belief in the resurrection?
http://www.joyfulheart.com/forums/index.php?showtopic=578

4. The Post-Resurrection Appearances of Jesus

The fourth important fact of Easter morning involves Jesus' appearances to several individuals and to ten of the disciples at the same time – all on the Sunday of the resurrection. Let me list these appearances:

1. Mary Magdalene (John 20:14-17; Matthew 28:9-10; Mark 16:9)

2. The other Mary (Matthew 28:9-10)

3. Peter (Luke 24:34; 1 Corinthians 15:5)

4. Cleopas and another disciple on the road to Emmaus on Sunday afternoon (Luke 24:13-35; Mark 16:12)

5. Disciples in Jerusalem on Sunday evening (Luke 24:36-43; Acts 1:4; John 20:19-23; Mark 16:14; 1 Corinthians 15:5)

6. Jesus also appeared to the disciples and others over a period of 40 days (Acts 1:3; 13:30-31).

7. Thomas and the other disciples, a week later (John 20:24-29)

8. Disciples in Galilee (Matthew 28:17)

9. Disciples (Peter, Thomas, Nathanael, James, John, and two others) while fishing on the Sea of Galilee (John 21:1-23)

10. 500 people at one time (1 Corinthians 15:6)

11. James, Jesus' brother, who later became the leader of the Jerusalem congregation (1 Corinthians 15:7)13

12. Disciples at the ascension (Matthew 28:51-52)

13. Paul (1 Corinthians 15:8), much later

The gospel writers and Paul are crystal clear that the risen Christ appeared to different individuals and groups of people at different times over a period of about 40 days. This pretty well shoots down the vision theory – all the alternate resurrection theories in fact. Paul indicates in 1 Corinthians 15:6 that most of whom are still living, though some have fallen asleep, in other words, he is claiming that eyewitnesses were living then –

---

[13] Fee, *1 Corinthians*, p. 731.

approximately 53-55 AD[14] – to whom Jesus had actually appeared. This was not some kind of secretive, hidden phenomenon, but was openly known and talked about in the early church.

Detractors claim there were no credible eyewitnesses. That is patently false; they are merely choosing to disbelieve any of the New Testament accounts.

5. The Spread of Christianity

The final important fact of the Easter account really took place after Easter Sunday in the rapid growth of the Church. Fifty days after the Passover on which Jesus was crucified was the feast of Pentecost in Jerusalem. On that day, the Holy Spirit fell upon 120 believers who were gathered praying. The rest is history, as they say. The Holy Spirit prompted the apostles to preach that Jesus had been raised from the dead – in the very city where he had been crucified and buried.

> "But God raised him from the dead, freeing him from the agony of death, because it was impossible for death to keep its hold on him." (Acts 2:24)

> "God has raised this Jesus to life, and we are all witnesses of the fact." (Acts 2:32)

> "You killed the author of life, but God raised him from the dead. We are witnesses of this." (Acts 3:15)

> "... Jesus Christ of Nazareth, whom you crucified but whom God raised from the dead...." (Acts 4:10)

> "With great power the apostles continued to testify to the resurrection of the Lord Jesus, and much grace was upon them all." (Acts 4:33)

> "The God of our fathers raised Jesus from the dead – whom you had killed by hanging him on a tree." (Acts 5:30)

The church grew to 3,000 on the day of Pentecost (Acts 2:41), then to 5,000 men (Acts 4:4), one fifth the population of Jerusalem, then the New Testament records that many among the priests of

---

[14] 1 Corinthians is dated in the Spring 53 to 55 AD (Fee, *1 Corinthians*, p. 15).

the city believed (Acts 6:7). When the Jews began heavy persecution against the Christian church, they preached the resurrection wherever they went.

> Peter in Caesarea: "They killed him by hanging him on a tree, but God raised him from the dead on the third day and caused him to be seen." (Acts 10:39-40)

> Paul in Pisidian Antioch: "They took him down from the tree and laid him in a tomb. But God raised him from the dead...." (Acts 13:29-30)

> Paul in Thessalonica: "... Explaining and proving that the Christ had to suffer and rise from the dead." (Acts 17:3)

> Paul in Athens: "[God] has given proof of this to all men by raising him from the dead." (Acts 17:31)

> Paul before King Agrippa and Governor Festus: "... That the Christ would suffer and, as the first to rise from the dead...." (Acts 26:23)

What galvanized a demoralized band of followers into fearless proclaimers of the resurrection? Within a generation or two, Christianity had spread to the farthest reaches of the Roman empire. By the early fourth century, Christianity had become the dominant religion – proclaiming the resurrection from the dead of Jesus Christ!

The easiest way to stop the spread of Christianity in Jerusalem would have been to produce Jesus' body. But Jesus' enemies were not able to convince the populace of Jerusalem that the resurrection was a fake. Too many people had seen Jesus after his resurrection. There were too many witnesses to the resurrection to shut down this new faith. As a result, Christianity mushroomed – first in Jerusalem, then Judea, Samaria, and finally to the uttermost parts of the earth (Acts 1:8).

Arguments from Silence

When you consider a theory that gospel accounts of the resurrection were concocted after the fact to prove something that didn't happen, observe several interesting facts about the accounts.

1. **Lack of Biblical quotations.** The rest of the gospels make constant reference to Old Testament scriptures that Christ fulfilled. Yes, Christ explains how his death and resurrection were foretold in Scripture (Luke 24:25-27, 46). The story is told plainly without embellishment.

2. **Lack of Christ appearing first to male disciples.** What we have is the testimony of Mary Magdalene, a woman, whose testimony wouldn't have much weight from a Jewish legal point of view. Yes, the scripture records later appearances to specific male disciples, but the detailed accounts concern women.

3. **Lack of emphasis on personal hope.** The future resurrection hope of the Christian isn't mentioned in these accounts. Rather, the emphasis seems to be: Jesus is risen, now you have work ahead of you!

4. **Lack of a portrait of Jesus.** Jesus is not depicted in these accounts as a heavenly being, radiant and shining. Rather he has a human body that is unusual.[15]

If, as some liberal Christian scholars claim, the accounts of the resurrection were concocted late by disciples creating a physical resurrection to support Christian faith, that the stories would pull out all the stops to prove the point. Instead, the accounts are told plainly as they occurred.

The Sufficiency of the Evidence

Taken individually, the various details of Jesus' resurrection would be powerful. But taking all the evidence together, the case for the resurrection is compelling. No alternate theory of the resurrection explains the remarkable facts of:

---

[15] These strange silences in the Biblical accounts are explored by Wright, *Resurrection*, pp. 599-608.

1. The empty tomb,
2. The undisturbed grave clothes,
3. The disciples' psychological state,
4. The post-resurrection appearances of Christ, and
5. The spread of Christianity.

What seems to some as too good to be true indeed is true. We all face death, but Christ's resurrection is the Good News that we Christians can proclaim to our world. Death is not the end. As he was raised, so we will be also!

Q4. Which of the various proofs for the resurrection seems the most compelling to you? Why? If you had a friend who wasn't sure about the resurrection, could you explain why you're sure that Jesus was raised from the dead?
http://www.joyfulheart.com/forums/index.php?showtopic=579

Prayer

Father, thank you for the strong assurances you have given us that Christ has been raised indeed! Strengthen your Church in this faith as well, that around the world we might proclaim the resurrection of Christ our Lord without embarrassment or hesitation. Teach us to tell the Good News! In Jesus' name, we pray. Amen.

Key Verses

"For what I received I passed on to you as of first importance : that Christ died for our sins according to the Scriptures, that he was buried, that he was raised on the third day according to the Scriptures, and that he appeared to Peter, and then to the Twelve. After that, he appeared to more than five hundred of the brothers at the same time, most of whom are still living, though some have fallen asleep. Then he appeared to James, then to all the apostles, and last of all he appeared to me also, as to one abnormally born." (1 Corinthians 15:3-8)

4. The Present-Day Significance of Christ's Resurrection

We've considered resurrection in the Old and New Testaments, studied the events of Jesus' resurrection on the third day, and examined the convincing proofs that Jesus is indeed risen from the dead. But those things are past events. What does the resurrection mean to us now?

It is very difficult to be comprehensive about the meaning of the resurrection. The resurrection is mentioned specifically in 18 of the 27 New Testament books and implied in the rest, so there are many verses that relate to this subject. However, as I survey the New Testament, four overarching themes stand out to me:

Ambrogio di Stefano Bergognone (Milanese painter, ca. 1460-1523), Christ Risen from the Tomb (c. 1490), National Gallery of Art, Washington, DC.

1. Jesus' Resurrection Is God's Seal of Approval on Jesus

2. Jesus' Resurrection Validates our Salvation

3. Jesus' Resurrection Typifies our Spiritual Union with Him

4. Jesus' Resurrection Is the Harbinger of our Own Resurrection on the Last Day

1. Jesus' Resurrection Is God's Seal of Approval on Jesus

The first theme is that Jesus' resurrection is God's vindication of Jesus' life, ministry, person, and divinity.

When Jesus died a criminal's death on the hill of Golgotha outside of Jerusalem, hope died with him. His disciples and many others had come to believe in him as the Messiah. Some even believed he was the Son of God, that is, divine. Then the scourge tore into his back, merciless nails were pounded through his hands and feet, his body was jerked erect as the cross was pulled vertical and dropped into its hole in the parched earth. For six hours he hung there and finally died. His disciples took his body down and tenderly buried him.

But that day a glorious movement of the Kingdom of God was buried, too. Or so it seemed. Then Easter morning God raised him from the dead. It was as if God was attesting to the authenticity of his Son, validating his teachings, and saying in the most unmistakably graphic terms what he had said in words at Jesus' Baptism: "This is my beloved Son, in whom I am well pleased" (Matthew 3:17). This was a strong element of early preaching in Jerusalem, which contrasted the Jews killing of Jesus with God's raising him:

> "God has raised this Jesus to life.... Therefore let all Israel be assured of this: **God has made this Jesus,** whom you crucified, **both Lord and Christ."** (Acts 2:32, 36)

> "The God of our fathers raised Jesus from the dead – whom you had killed by hanging him on a tree. **God exalted him to his own right hand as Prince and Savior** that he might give repentance and forgiveness of sins to Israel." (Acts 5:30-31)

> "For he has set a day when **he will judge the world** with justice by the man he has appointed. He has given proof[1] of this to all men by raising him from the dead." (Acts 17:31)

---

[1] *Pistis* here has the older classical meaning of guarantee or assurance in the sense of "a pledge or oath with the two nuances of trustworthiness and proof" (Rudolf Bultmann, *pisteuō, ktl.,* TDNT 6:197-228; cf. Robertson, *Word Pictures, in loc.*).

> "[He] was declared with power to be the **Son of God** by his resurrection from the dead: Jesus Christ our Lord." (Romans 1:4)

It is one thing for claims to be made about who Jesus was. But God set his own seal upon him at the resurrection validating those claims. After all, if God has raised him from the dead, who but a fool would try to prove that he is a mere man.

Q1. What kind of credibility would Jesus' ministry have had if he were not raised from the dead, especially when he predicted it ahead of time? In what way is the resurrection God's seal of approval on him?
http://www.joyfulheart.com/forums/index.php?showtopic=580

2. Jesus' Resurrection Validates our Salvation

A related theme is more specific, that Jesus' resurrection validates our own salvation. I've often pondered over a passage in Romans:

> "He was delivered over to death for (*dia*) our sins and was raised to life for (*dia*) our justification." (Romans 4:25)

A simplistic way to construe this is to assume that Jesus' death on the cross atoned for our sins, while in a separate event Jesus' resurrection took care of declaring us pardoned and blameless. The key word in this verse is the preposition *dia*, used in both clauses, which can mean either because of (retrospective) or with a view to, to bring about (prospective).[2]

---

[2] William Sanday and Arthur C. Headlam, *A Critical and Exegetical Commentary on the Epistle to the Romans* (International Critical Commentary; Fifth Edition; Edinburgh: T&T Clark, 1902), p. 116; John Murray, *The Epistle to the Romans* (New International Commentary on the New Testament; Eerdmans, 1959, one volume edition 1968), p. 154-157; C.K. Barrett, *A Commentary on the Epistle to the Romans* (Harpers New Testament Commentaries; Harper & Row, 1957), p. 100; Leon Morris, *The Epistle to the Romans* (Pillar Commentary; Eerdmans, 1988), pp. 214-216.

But I don't think Paul sees these as separate events, but both part of the whole, in a construction reminiscent of Hebrew synoptic parallelism or progressive parallelism that we often see in Hebrew poetry. What is sure is that the resurrection here validates our salvation and completes it. Indeed, without the resurrection, Jesus' death would mean ... only that he was dead. As Paul indicates in the strongest possible terms:

> "13 If there is no resurrection of the dead, then not even Christ has been raised. 14 And if Christ has not been raised, our preaching is useless and so is your faith. 15 More than that, we are then found to be false witnesses about God, for we have testified about God that he raised Christ from the dead. But he did not raise him if in fact the dead are not raised. 16 For if the dead are not raised, then Christ has not been raised either. 17 And **if Christ has not been raised, your faith is futile; you are still in your sins**. 18 Then those also who have fallen asleep in Christ are lost. 19 If only for this life we have hope in Christ, we are to be pitied more than all men." (1 Corinthians 15:13-19)

It is because Christ has been raised from the dead that we have assurance or proof that God has completed our salvation. Because God vindicated Jesus by raising him from the dead, we know that his promises of forgiveness of sins are true, that we have been saved, rescued, delivered. Several times the resurrection is referred to as the basis of our confidence in salvation:

> "Who will bring any charge against those whom God has chosen? It is God who justifies. Who is he that condemns? Christ Jesus, who died – more than that, who was **raised to life** – is at the right hand of God and is also interceding for us." (Romans 8:33-34)

> "Through him you believe in God, who **raised him from the dead** and glorified him, and so your faith and hope are in God." (1 Peter 1:21)

> "Therefore, since we have a great high priest **who has gone through the heavens**,[3] Jesus the Son of God.... Let us then approach the throne of grace with confidence, so that we may receive mercy and find grace to help us in our time of need." (Hebrews 4:14, 16)

Because he lives, we have confidence that our salvation is not a pipe dream based on empty hopes, but a firm expectation based on Jesus' resurrection from the dead.

Q2. In what way does Christ's resurrection somehow validate that we are saved and forgiven by God? If we didn't believe Christ had been actually raised from the dead, how might we have doubts about our salvation?
http://www.joyfulheart.com/forums/index.php?showtopic=581

3. Jesus' Resurrection Typifies our Spiritual Union with Him

A third theme in the New Testament that expresses Jesus' death and resurrection as a kind of analogy to our spiritual life. This gets a bit complex, so hang in here with me. Paul is arguing that we must stop living in sin:

> "Don't you know that all of us who were baptized into Christ Jesus were baptized into his death? We were therefore **buried** with him through baptism into death in order that, just as Christ was **raised** from the dead through the glory of the Father, we too may live a new life. If we have been united[4] with him like this in his **death**, we will certainly also be united with him in his **resurrection**." (Romans 6:3-5)

---

[3] The phrase "gone through the heavens," of course, refers specifically to Jesus' ascension and glorification at the right hand of the Father. It assumes, of course, the resurrection that preceded it.

[4] "United" (NIV, NRSV), "planted together" (KJV) is *symphytos*, from *symphyō*, "planted together, born together with, of joint origin, then grown together, united with" (Thayer, 2).

Here Paul sees the act of baptism as a type of Jesus' own death and resurrection, and a vivid reminder of our union with him in both his death and resurrection. See the parallels:

Christ	Death and burial	Resurrection
Baptism	Immersed in the water	Brought out of the water
Believers	United with him in his death	Shall be united with him (in the future) in his resurrection

In Colossians we find a similar figure:

> "... Having been buried with him in baptism and raised with him through your faith in the power of God, who raised him from the dead." (Colossians 2:12)

As A.T. Robertson puts it,

> "Baptism is a picture of the past and of the present and a prophecy of the future, the matchless preacher of the new life in Christ."[5]

Peter, too, carries on this theme of resurrection as a symbol of regeneration:

> "In his great mercy he has given us **new birth** into a living hope through the **resurrection** of Jesus Christ from the dead...." (1 Peter 1:3)

In a number of passages, Paul speaks of being *co-crucified* with Christ and *co-resurrected* with Christ, beginning with the Romans 6 baptismal passage we just looked at, which continues:

> "6 For we know that our old self was crucified with him.... 8 Now if we **died** with Christ, we believe that we will also **live** with him.... 11 In the same way, count yourselves **dead** to sin but **alive** to God in Christ Jesus." (Romans 6:6, 8, 11)

Elsewhere, Paul repeats this theme, with the same ethical imperative to live out our new life with integrity:

---

[5] Robertson, *Word Pictures*, on Romans 6:5. In a difficult passage, 1 Peter 3:21 also refers to this association with baptism, resurrection, and new life.

> "I have been **crucified with Christ** and I no longer live, but Christ lives in me. The life I live in the body, I live by faith in the Son of God, who loved me and gave himself for me." (Galatians 5:20)

> "Since, then, you have been **raised with Christ**, set your hearts on things above, where Christ is seated at the right hand of God. Set your minds on things above, not on earthly things. For you died, and your life is now hidden with Christ in God. When Christ, who is your life, appears, then you also will appear with him in glory." (Colossians 3:1-4)

We also see Jesus' resurrection and subsequent ascension to glory at the Father's right hand as a type of our own spiritual life:

> "That power is like the working of his mighty strength, which he exerted in Christ when **he raised him from the dead** and seated him at his right hand in the heavenly realms...." (Ephesians 1:19b-20)

> "[1] As for you, you were **dead** in your transgressions and sins.... [4b] But because of his great love for us, God, who is rich in mercy, [5] **made us alive** with Christ even when we were dead in transgressions – it is by grace you have been saved. [6] And God **raised us up with Christ** and seated us with him in the heavenly realms in Christ Jesus...." (Ephesians 2:1, 4b-6)

At Christ's right hand we share his power and privileges in the spiritual world. Our being co-raised with Christ typifies the grace of God to us. This may be a spiritual expression, but if you have tasted of its reality, then you know something of the wonder of what Paul is expressing here.

Q3. How does Christ's death and resurrection provide an analogy for baptism according to Romans 6:3-5 and Colossians 2:12? According to Ephesians 2:4-6, while being raised with Christ is still spiritual, not physical, in what way does this union impart real spiritual power?

http://www.joyfulheart.com/forums/index.php?showtopic=582

4. Jesus' Resurrection Is the Harbinger of our Own Resurrection on the Last Day

Our resurrection is not only a spiritual metaphor. The New Testament is abundantly clear that Christ's resurrection is a harbinger or precursor of our own resurrection at the Last Day. Well study this in greater detail in the final lesson in this series, but for now, let's observe that in Christ's resurrection is the promise of our own. Of the many New Testament promises along this line, here are a few:

> "By his power God raised the Lord from the dead, and he will raise us also." (1 Corinthians 6:14)

> "... The one who raised the Lord Jesus from the dead will also raise us with Jesus and present us with you in his presence." (2 Corinthians 4:14)

Christ's resurrection from the dead is the first, the prototype resurrection, but it is not to be the last. He is the **firstfruits** of those who have fallen asleep (1 Corinthians 15:20), the **firstborn** from the dead (Revelation 1:5) He opens up the way for the rest of us:

> "I am the Living One; I was **dead**, and behold I am **alive for ever and ever**! And I hold the keys of death and Hades." (Revelation 1:18)

That is our promise, that Christ's resurrection is the focus of our own hope for eternal life. Not just some kind of disembodied immortal soul, but a bodily resurrection like Christ's own. As Job fervently hoped nearly three thousand years ago.

> "I know that my Redeemer lives,
> and that in the end he will stand upon the earth.
> And after my skin has been destroyed,
> yet in my flesh I will see God;
> I myself will see him
> with my own eyes – I, and not another.
> How my heart yearns within me!" (Job 19:25-27)

Q4. What assurance do you have that you will be physically resurrected rather than experience disembodied immortality? What does it mean that Jesus is the firstfruits (1 Corinthians 15:20) and firstborn (Revelation 1:5) from the dead?
http://www.joyfulheart.com/forums/index.php?showtopic=583

Indeed, the resurrection of Christ is a central theme in the New Testament. Because of his resurrection we are assured:

- That he is indeed the divine Son of God,
- That our sins are forgiven and our salvation is secure,
- That we are united with him and the power of his resurrection, and
- That we too will be bodily raised from the dead as he was.

For the Apostle Paul, the resurrection was an integral part of his fervent prayer for the present and his longing for the future:

> "I want to know Christ and the power of his resurrection and the fellowship of sharing in his sufferings, becoming like him in his death, and so, somehow, to attain to the resurrection from the dead." (Philippians 3:10-11)

The Encouragement of Resurrection

What effect is Christ's resurrection and the hope of our own resurrection to have on us Christians? Paul concludes 1 Corinthians 15 with these words, beginning with a therefore that sums up the entire chapter's hope of resurrection:

> "Therefore, my beloved brethren, be steadfast, immovable, always abounding in the work of the Lord, knowing that in the Lord your labor is not in vain." (1 Corinthians 15:58, RSV)

You may have faced – or be facing – horrendous challenges as you seek to follow Christ in this life. Don't become discouraged. You may be feeling that your body is giving out, falling apart.

Don't quit. On the solid hope of the resurrection to come, Paul exhorts us with these words.

Steadfast is *hedraios*, "pertaining to being firmly or solidly in place, firm, steadfast."[6]

Immovable is *ametakinētos*, "unshifting, unchanging, immovable."[7]

The words of a great African American spiritual develop this theme from Psalm 1:

> "I shall not be, I shall not be moved,
> I shall not be, I shall not be moved,
> Just like a tree planted by the water, Lord,
> I shall not be moved!"

Paul exhorted the Colossian believers to: "Continue in your faith, established and firm, not moved from the hope held out in the gospel" (Colossians 1:23). Don't be shaken by the world that is crashing and burning around you. "Let nothing move you!" (1 Corinthians 15:58, NIV).

The next phrase is **always abounding in the work of the Lord.** Abounding is *perisseuō*, "to be in abundance, abound." With regards to wealth, the word denotes, "be extremely rich or abundant, overflow." With regards to people serving Christ, it means, "be outstanding, be prominent, excel."[8]

In our weariness, in our times of discouragement and despair, we are to remember whose work this is – the Lords! Paul then mentions your **labor** (*kopos*), "engagement in activity that is burdensome, work, labor, toil"[9] – and that sometimes describes our work for the Lord. But two phrases modify labor here and make all the difference:

[6] *Hedraios*, BDAG 276.
[7] *Ametakinētos*, BDAG 53.
[8] *Perisseuō*, BDAG 805.
[9] *Kopos*, BDAG 558-559, 2.

1. **Not in vain**. Kenos means empty, which means here pertaining to being without purpose or result, in vain.[10] Your work is not empty, not in vain. Why? The next phrase explains that it is.

2. **In the Lord**. It isn't your work, but the Lords work. It isn't your labors, but the task to which he, the Lord of the Harvest, has set you to do for him. No matter that things don't always come together. Your work counts because it is his work, conducted for him in obedience to him. Others may discount it, but he doesn't forget. Your labor is in the Lord.

My dear friend, Christ is risen! And the promise of resurrection is yours also. Your work, as small as it may seem sometimes, is in the Lord and valued by him. So your mission, should you choose to accept it, is to remain steadfast, immovable, always abounding in the work of the Lord. Why? Christ the Risen One is coming and when he comes we shall rise from the dead in glory! It will be worth it!

What is the meaning of the resurrection for us today? Bill and Gloria Gaither put it rather clearly in their popular song:

"Because He lives I can face tomorrow
Because He lives all fear is gone
Because I know He holds the future
And life is worth the living
Just because He lives."[11]

Q5. (1 Corinthians 15:58) What does being steadfast and immovable have to do with the hope of the resurrection? *Why* is our labor not in vain in the Lord?
http://www.joyfulheart.com/forums/index.php?showtopic=584

---

[10] *Kenos*, BDAG 539, 3.
[11] "Because He Lives," words and music by William J. and Gloria Gaither (© 1971, William J. Gaither, Inc.; Gaither Copyright Management).

Prayer

Father, thank you for the joy, assurance, and hope that we believers can have through the resurrection. Bring it even sharper into focus for us as we seek to know you better in the power of Christ's resurrection. In Jesus' name, we pray. Amen.

Key Verses

"God has raised this Jesus to life…. Therefore let all Israel be assured of this: God has made this Jesus, whom you crucified, both Lord and Christ." (Acts 2:32, 36)

"Don't you know that all of us who were baptized into Christ Jesus were baptized into his death? We were therefore buried with him through baptism into death in order that, just as Christ was raised from the dead through the glory of the Father, we too may live a new life. If we have been united with him like this in his death, we will certainly also be united with him in his resurrection." (Romans 6:3-5)

"And if Christ has not been raised, your faith is futile; you are still in your sins." (1 Corinthians 15:17)

5. The Christian Hope of Resurrection at the Last Day

As you prepare to study this lesson, read again 1 Corinthians 15 and 1 Thessalonians 4:13-18.

Jesus was raised from the dead on the third day, breaking the hold that death had on mankind. He is the firstborn from the dead (Revelation 1:5; Colossians 1:18), the firstfruits of those who

Luca Signorelli (c. 1450-1532), "Angel Blowing Horn at the Resurrection on the Last Day", detail from "Resurrection of the Flesh" (1499-1502), Fresco, Chapel of San Brizio, Duomo, Orvieto, Italy.

have fallen asleep (1 Corinthians 15:20). He is the first to be resurrected eternally, but not the last. Jesus clearly taught that on the Last Day, both the righteous and the unrighteous will be raised, the righteous to eternal life, and the unrighteous to eternal condemnation (John 5:28-29; Daniel 12:2-3; Acts 24:15).

Rapture vs. Resurrection

I've heard a lot of Christians talk about the rapture (a word that doesn't actually occur in the New Testament) but far fewer talk about the resurrection (which is mentioned many times). The word rapture comes from the Latin noun *raptus*, which means, a carrying off, a concept referred to in 1 Thessalonians 4:17. Clearly, the rapture of the saints and the resurrection of the righteous are one and the same event. Jesus himself talked about this great resurrection in terms of gathering. In a moment well look at several passages of scripture describing the order of Christ's return, but first observe the elements in the accounts:

1. The **appearance of Christ** in the heavens,
2. The angels **trumpet call** summoning all God's people,
3. **Gathering of his people**, dead and alive (the quick and the dead) (Matthew 13:24-30, 37-43, 47-50; 25:31-46; 2 Thessalonians 2:1)
4. **Resurrection** of those who are dead *and*

    a. **Changing** into resurrection bodies of those alive at that time.

    b. Appearing before God's **judgment** (Revelation 20:11-13)

5. **Entering into glory**

These things are mentioned in a number of places in the New Testament, but most completely in the following four passages:

> "At that time the sign of the Son of Man will appear in the sky, and all the nations of the earth will mourn. They will see the Son of Man coming on the clouds of the sky, with power and great glory. And he will send his angels with a loud trumpet call, and they will **gather**[1] **his elect** from the four winds, from one end of the heavens to the other." (Matthew 24:30-31, parallel Mark 13:27)

> "Listen, I tell you a mystery: We will not all sleep, but we will all be changed – in a flash, in the twinkling of an eye, at the last trumpet. For the trumpet will sound, the dead will be **raised imperishable**,[2] and we will be **changed**."[3] (1 Corinthians 15:51-52)

---

[1] *Episynagō*," to bring together, gather (together)" (BDAG 382). See also the noun in, "Concerning the coming of our Lord Jesus Christ and our being gathered (*episynagōgē*) to him..." (2 Thessalonians 2:1).

[2] *Aphthartos*, "pertaining to imperviousness to corruption and death, imperishable, incorruptible, immortal," the adjective of *aphtharsia* (1 Corinthians 15:42), see footnote 8 below.

[3] *Allassō*, "to make something other or different, change alter" (BDAG 45-46, 1).

"For the Lord himself will come down from heaven, with a loud command, with the voice of the archangel and with the trumpet call of God, and the dead in Christ will rise first. After that, we who are still alive and are left will be **caught up together**[4] with them in the clouds to meet the Lord in the air. And so we will be with the Lord forever." (1 Thessalonians 4:16-17)

"Then I saw a great white throne and him who was seated on it. Earth and sky fled from his presence, and there was no place for them. And I saw the dead, great and small, standing before the throne, and books were opened. Another book was opened, which is the book of life. The dead were judged according to what they had done as recorded in the books. **The sea gave up the dead that were in it, and death and Hades gave up the dead that were in them,** and each person was judged according to what he had done." (Revelation 20:11-13; see also Romans 14:10; 2 Corinthians 5:10)

Q1. What is the word used in the Bible instead of rapture? When will the resurrection take place in relation to Christ's return? In relation to judgment? In relation to glory? (This is *not* the place to debate various theories of the rapture and the millennium. Be kind and loving!)
http://www.joyfulheart.com/forums/index.php?showtopic=585

In Heaven Prior to the Resurrection

In 1 Thessalonians 4:17 above we see both the resurrection of the dead (and the dead in Christ will rise first) and the rapture of those Christians still alive (we who are still alive and are left will be caught up together with them). Where have the dead been during this time? Verse 14 is rather clear: We believe that **God will bring with Jesus those who have fallen asleep in him.** They

---

[4] *Harpazō,* "to grab or seize suddenly so as to remove control, snatch/take away" (BDAG 134, 2.b.). The Latin Vulgate translation uses *rapio,* "seize, carry off by force," related to our English words "rapture" and "rape."

have been in the presence of God from the instant of their death until the resurrection.

Occasionally you may hear the doctrine of soul sleep, that Christians who die are asleep until the resurrection, when suddenly they awake – unaware of the interval in time – and are raised from the dead at the Last Day. Sleep is sometimes used as a euphemism for death in the New Testament. But soul sleep is not taught in the Bible. The scriptures are clear that at death, Christians are with Christ instantly. Consider Paul's words:

> "I am torn between the two: I desire to depart and **be with Christ**, which is **better by far**; but it is more necessary for you that I remain in the body." (Philippians 1:23-24)

> "We are confident, I say, and would prefer to be away from the body and **at home**[5] **with the Lord**." (2 Corinthians 5:8)

So at the moment of death, we are ushered into the presence of God. The Book of Revelation twice mentions saints in heaven awaiting the resurrection.

> "I saw under the altar the souls of those who had been slain because of the word of God and the testimony they had maintained. They called out in a loud voice, 'How long, Sovereign Lord, holy and true, until you judge the inhabitants of the earth and avenge our blood?' Then each of them was given a white robe, and they were told to wait a little longer, until the number of their fellow servants and brothers who were to be killed as they had been was completed." (Revelation 6:9-11)

The other mention is the 144,000, wearing white robes and were holding palm branches in their hands (7:9), worshiping the Lamb. These are they who have come out of the great tribulation (7:14). I think it's likely that these are two different pictures of the same group, though, of course, that's hotly debated.

The point is that there is a place for us with God, for Jesus told his disciples:

---

[5] *Endēmeō*, "to be in a familiar place, to be at home" (BDAG 332).

> "In my Father's house are many rooms; if it were not so, I would have told you. I am going there to prepare a place for you. And if I go and prepare a place for you, I will come back and take you to be with me that you also may be where I am." (John 14:2-3)

Q2. (Philippians 1:23-24; 2 Corinthians 5:8) According to these verses, where will Christians be immediately after death? Where do we await the resurrection?

http://www.joyfulheart.com/forums/index.php?showtopic=586

Redemption and Glorification

Getting into heaven will satisfy me, you might be saying. You can have this old body. That may be so, but God has a plan not only for your immortal soul, but also your body. We see several words that describe this in the New Testament:

Redemption of our bodies. Paul writes,

> "We ourselves ... groan inwardly as we wait eagerly for **our adoption as sons, the redemption of our bodies.** For in this hope we were saved." (Romans 8:23-24a)

Redemption (*apolytrōsis*) means literally, "'making free' by payment of a ransom."[6] Christ's redemption is not only spiritual, but holistic, physical. In some sense, the completion of the promises of God to us (such as adoption as sons) await the resurrection at the Last Day.

Glorification. A number of passages associate being glorified with receiving the resurrection body: It is sown in dishonor, it is **raised in glory** (1 Corinthians 15:43; also Romans 8:17, 30; 2 Corinthians 3:18; 4:17; Philippians 3:21; Colossians 1:27; 3:4; 2 Thessalonians 2:14; 2 Timothy 2:10; Hebrews 2:10;) This glory was also spoken concerning Jesus (Luke 24:26; John 7:39; 12:16, 23; 13:31; Acts 3:13; Colossians 3:4; 1 Timothy 3:16; Hebrews 2:9; 1

---

[6] *Apolytrōsis*, BDAG 117, 2a.

Peter 1:11, 21). There seems to be a special sense in which our final entering into Christ's glory will follow our resurrection.

Corruptible vs. Incorruptible, Natural vs. Spiritual Bodies

Probably the most important passage teaching about the resurrection is 1 Corinthians 15. Here Paul gives a number of contrasts between the characteristics of the natural body and those of the resurrection body.

> "[35] But someone may ask, 'How are the dead raised? **With what kind of body will they come?'** ... [42] So will it be with the resurrection of the dead. The body that is sown is **perishable**, it is raised **imperishable;** [43] it is sown in **dishonor**, it is raised in **glory**; it is sown in **weakness**, it is raised in **power;** [44] it is sown a **natural body**, it is raised a **spiritual body**." (1 Corinthians 15:35, 42-44)

We see several pairs of words in this passage:

Corruptible - Incorruptible. Our physical bodies are perishable, corruptible, *phthora*, "a breakdown of organic matter, dissolution, deterioration, corruption" in the world of nature. Then, "the state of being perishable."[7] But our bodies in the resurrection will be just the opposite – imperishable, incorruptible (*aphtharsia*).[8]

Edward Burne-Jones (Pre-Raphaelite English painter, 1833-1893), "Last Judgment" (1896). West Window, St. Philips Cathedral, Birmingham, UK.

Dishonor - Glory. Our physical

---

[7] *Phthora*, BDAG 1054-1055, 1.

[8] *Aphtharsia*, "the state of not being subject to decay/dissolution/interruption" (BDAG 155).

bodies are characterized by dishonor, *atimia*, "dishonor, ignominy, disgrace," used here of the unseemliness and offensiveness of a dead body.[9] The contrast is a resurrection characterized by glory, *doxa*, "the condition of being bright or shining, brightness, splendor, radiance."[10]

Weakness - Power. The physical body, especially one that is showing its age, is weak. The Greek noun is *astheneia*, which refers to both sickness, disease and physical weakness – incapacity or experience of limitation.[11] By contrast the resurrection body is raised in power, *dynamis*, power, might, strength, force, capability.[12]

Natural - Spiritual. Paul describes the natural body with the adjective *psychikos*, from *psychē*, "soul, life," means here specifically, "pertaining to the life of the natural world and whatever belongs to it, in contrast to the realm of experience whose central characteristic is *pneuma*, natural, unspiritual, worldly."[13] Here it is translated natural (NIV, KJV) or physical (NRSV). The resurrection body is described as *pneumatikos*, having to do with the (divine spirit).[14] This doesn't mean that people in the resurrection are spirits without a body. Jesus wasn't. But it means that the resurrection body has a spiritual dimension as Jesus' resurrection body did, able to operate in the spiritual realm as well as the physical.

Q3. What does the phrase "redemption of our bodies" (Romans 8:23-24) tell us about our resurrection? What words in 1 Corinthians 15:42-44 describe our resurrection bodies?
http://www.joyfulheart.com/forums/index.php?showtopic=587

---

[9] *Atimia*, Thayer.
[10] *Doxa*, BDAG 256-258, 1b.
[11] *Astheneia*, BDAG 142, 2a.
[12] *Dynamis*, BDAG 262-263, 1.
[13] *Psychikos*, BDAG 1100.
[14] *Pneumatikos*, BDAG 837, 2.

What Is Our Resurrection Body Going to Be Like?

Just what is our resurrection body going to be like? Consider these passages:

> "Dear friends, now we are children of God, and what we will be has not yet been made known. But we know that when he appears, **we shall be like him**, for we shall see him as he is." (1 John 3:2)

> "[The Lord Jesus], who, by the power that enables him to bring everything under his control, will transform our lowly bodies so that they will be **like his glorious body**." (Philippians 3:21)

> "And just as we have borne the likeness of the earthly man, so shall we **bear the likeness of the man from heaven**." (1 Corinthians 15:49)

Our resurrection bodies will be like Jesus' resurrection body. While we can't be certain of all that means for us, Jesus' body was described as flesh and bones (Luke 24:39c) – though, of course, it is more than that (1 Corinthians 15:50)! Jesus' body could eat (Luke 24:42-43; Acts 1:4), be touched (Matthew 28:9; Luke 24:39b), could walk and talk (Luke 24:15), and be recognized by others – when he wanted to be (Matthew 28:9; Luke 24:16, 31; John 20:14-16, 20; 21:4, 12). In these respects, it was able to relate to the physical world like a normal physical body.

But it was not limited to the physical world. Jesus could enter locked doors (John 20:19, 26) disappear (Luke 24:31) and appear (Luke 24:36) at will. Our resurrection bodies will be incorruptible (1 Corinthians 15:42), glorified (1 Corinthians 15:43a), powerful (1 Corinthians 15:43b), and able to navigate in the spiritual realm (1 Corinthians 15:44).

Jesus' wounds were still visible in his renewed body (Luke 24:39-40; John 20:20, 25-27). Does that mean that our resurrection bodies will bear the scars, wounds, and sicknesses of our earthly struggle? No. Jesus' body seems to be a special case so his disciples would not mistake who he was. We expect that our bodies will be raised to an appearance that is in the full strength of health and beauty. Nevertheless, physical beauty will no longer have the sexual implications that it does now, since in the resurrection, marriage and sexuality no longer have meaning (Luke 20:34-36). These are spiritual bodies, no longer mortal. Jesus said: "They can no longer die, for they are like the angels" (Luke 20:36).

Why Will We Have Resurrection Bodies?

For some, who are quite happy with heaven – thank you very much – resurrection bodies may seem unnecessary. Why go to all this trouble? they ask. Surely, resurrection is the final victory over death. But we probably don't know the full answer. Nevertheless, I have often pondered these verses:

> "That day will bring about the destruction of the heavens by fire, and the elements will melt in the heat. But in keeping with his promise we are looking forward to a **new heaven and a new earth**, the home of righteousness." (2 Peter 3:12-13)

> "Then I saw a **new heaven and a new earth**, for the first heaven and the first earth had passed away... He who was seated on the throne said, 'I am making everything new!'" (Revelation 21:1, 5)

> "You have made them to be a kingdom and priests to serve our God, and **they will reign on the earth**." (Revelation 5:10)

What is life going to be like in the new heavens and new earth? We don't know. But we do know that in the resurrection we will have bodies that are capable of navigating on earth as well as heaven, and we may have some role in both places as we reign, that is administer the rule of the Kingdom of God, on earth. We'll see!

Q4. What will our resurrection bodies be like? Why do you think we will be given resurrection bodies? What is the point?
http://www.joyfulheart.com/forums/index.php?showtopic=588

Getting All the Right Molecules Restored

Clearly, Jesus' resurrection body had a continuity with his physical body. After the resurrection he was recognized (when he wanted to be) and his wounds were visible as a sign that it indeed was he.

For us, frankly, by the time Jesus comes there may not be a lot left to resurrect. For this reason, some Christians have resisted cremation so that at least some bones are left rather than ashes. To a whimsical mind, this presents all sorts of questions. What if someone is buried at sea and his molecules end up as part of the food chain in another human being? But this whole approach becomes silly. Wayne Grudem puts it this way:

> "Whatever remains in the grave from our own physical bodies will be taken by God and transformed and used to make a new resurrection body. But the details of how that will happen remain unclear to us."[15]

Death Is Not the Victor

The point is that physical death is not the victor. Paul writes, The last enemy to be destroyed is death (1 Corinthians 15:26). Resurrection of the body on the Last Day underscores the completeness with which God is restoring us to his original intent, our wasted world to the Garden of Eden and a New Heavens and a New Earth where righteousness dwell (2 Peter 3:13; Revelation 21:1, 5; Isaiah 65:17-19; 66:22).

I've conducted many funerals in my lifetime. Many times as I have stood in cemeteries surveying all the graves around me, I've thought: This will be a wonderful, wild place to be when Christ returns and raises the bodies lying here to resurrection life!

The resurrection is the sign of victory and glory. Death is not the end. Death does not have the last word. Your Christian loved ones are with Christ right now in spirit. But one day, at Christ's

---

[15] Grudem, *Systematic Theology*, p. 833.

return, their bodies will rise, be reunited with their spirits, and live triumphant with Christ.

> "Listen, I will tell you a mystery! We will not all die, but we will all be changed, in a moment, in the twinkling of an eye, at the last trumpet. For the trumpet will sound, and the dead will be raised imperishable, and we will be changed. For this perishable body must put on imperishability, and this mortal body must put on immortality... Thanks be to God, who gives us the victory through our Lord Jesus Christ!" (1 Corinthians 15:51-53, 57, NRSV)

Come soon, Lord Jesus!

Q5. Why should Christians look forward to the events surrounding our resurrection? Why do you think Christians have largely lost this as their active expectation and hope? What should be done to reclaim these truths?
http://www.joyfulheart.com/forums/index.php?showtopic=589

Prayer

Father, thank you for the confidence we have of victory over death through our Lord Jesus Christ. Implant in us afresh a living faith in the resurrection of Jesus Christ our Lord and a living hope of our own resurrection on the Last Day. In Jesus' triumphant name, we pray. Amen.

Key Verses

> "Listen, I tell you a mystery: We will not all sleep, but we will all be changed – in a flash, in the twinkling of an eye, at the last trumpet. For the trumpet will sound, the dead will be raised imperishable, and we will be changed." (1 Corinthians 15:51-52)

> "For the Lord himself will come down from heaven, with a loud command, with the voice of the archangel and with the trumpet call of God, and the dead in Christ will rise first. After that, we who are still alive and are left will be caught up together with

them in the clouds to meet the Lord in the air. And so we will be with the Lord forever." (1 Thessalonians 4:16-17)

Appendix 1. Parallel Accounts of the Resurrection (NIV)

The following parallels are from the New International Version. If you'd like to print this out, it is available online at www.jesuswalk.com/resurrection/parallel-accounts-of-the-resurrection.pdf

Matthew 28:1-10	Mark 16:1-8 and 9-14 (longer end)	Luke 24:1-44	John 20:1-29
1 After the Sabbath, at dawn on the first day of the week, Mary Magdalene and the other Mary went to look at the tomb.	1 When the Sabbath was over, Mary Magdalene, Mary the mother of James, and Salome bought spices so that they might go to anoint Jesus' body. 2 Very early on the first day of the week, just after sunrise, they were on their way to the tomb	1 On the first day of the week, very early in the morning, the women took the spices they had prepared and went to the tomb. 10 It was Mary Magdalene, Joanna, Mary the mother of James, and the others with them....	1 Early on the first day of the week, while it was still dark, Mary Magdalene went to the tomb
	3 and they asked each other, Who will roll the stone away from the entrance of the tomb?		1b and saw that the stone had been removed from the entrance.
2 There was a violent earthquake, for an angel of the Lord came down from			

heaven and, going to the tomb, rolled back the stone and sat on it. ³ His appearance was like lightning, and his clothes were white as snow. ⁴ The guards were so afraid of him that they shook and became like dead men.			
	⁴ But when they looked up, they saw that the stone, which was very large, had been rolled away.	² They found the stone rolled away from the tomb, ³ but when they entered, they did not find the body of the Lord Jesus.	
	⁵ As they entered the tomb, they saw a young man dressed in a white robe sitting on the right side, and they were alarmed.	⁴ While they were wondering about this, suddenly two men in clothes that gleamed like lightning stood beside them. ⁵ In their fright the women bowed down with their faces to the ground,	
⁵ The angel said to the women, "Do not be afraid, for I	⁶ "Don't be alarmed," he said. "You are looking	⁵ᵇ but the men said to them, "Why do you	

know that you are looking for Jesus, who was crucified. 6 He is not here; he has risen, just as he said. Come and see the place where he lay."	for Jesus the Nazarene, who was crucified. He has risen! He is not here. See the place where they laid him."	look for the living among the dead? 6 He is not here; he has risen!"	
		6b Remember how he told you, while he was still with you in Galilee: 7 'The Son of Man must be delivered into the hands of sinful men, be crucified and on the third day be raised again. '" 8 Then they remembered his words.	
7 "Then go quickly and tell his disciples: He has risen from the dead and is going ahead of you into Galilee. There you will see him. Now I have told you."	7 "But go, tell his disciples and Peter, 'He is going ahead of you into Galilee. There you will see him, just as he told you. '"		
8 So the women hurried away from the tomb, afraid yet filled with joy, and ran to tell his	8 Trembling and bewildered, the women went out and fled from the tomb. They said nothing to	9 When they came back from the tomb, they told all these things to the Eleven and to all the others.	2 So she came running to Simon Peter and the other disciple, the one Jesus loved, and said, "They

disciples.	anyone, because they were afraid.	¹⁰ It was Mary Magdalene, Joanna, Mary the mother of James, and the others with them who told this to the apostles. ¹¹ But they did not believe the women, because their words seemed to them like nonsense.	have taken the Lord out of the tomb, and we don't know where they have put him!"
⁹ Suddenly Jesus met them. "Greetings," he said. They came to him, clasped his feet and worshiped him. ¹⁰ Then Jesus said to them, "Do not be afraid. Go and tell my brothers to go to Galilee; there they will see me."	⁹ When Jesus rose early on the first day of the week, he appeared first to Mary Magdalene, out of whom he had driven seven demons. ¹⁰ She went and told those who had been with him and who were mourning and weeping. ¹¹ When they heard that Jesus was alive and that she had seen him, they did not believe it.		¹¹ but Mary stood outside the tomb crying. As she wept, she bent over to look into the tomb ¹² and saw two angels in white, seated where Jesus body had been, one at the head and the other at the foot. ¹³ They asked her, "Woman, why are you crying?" "They have taken my Lord away", she said, "and I don't know where they have put him." ¹⁴ At this, she turned around and saw Jesus standing there,

			but she did not realize that it was Jesus.
			[15] "Woman, he said, why are you crying? Who is it you are looking for?" Thinking he was the gardener, she said, "Sir, if you have carried him away, tell me where you have put him, and I will get him."
			[16] Jesus said to her, "Mary." She turned toward him and cried out in Aramaic, "Rabboni!" (which means Teacher).
			[17] Jesus said, "Do not hold on to me, for I have not yet returned to the Father. Go instead to my brothers and tell them, I am returning to my Father and your Father, to my God and your God."
			[18] Mary Magdalene went to the disciples with the news: "I have seen the Lord!" And she

			told them that he had said these things to her.
(vss. 11-15, guards report to the chief priests and are bribed to lie)			
		12 Peter, however, got up and ran to the tomb. Bending over, he saw the strips of linen lying by themselves, and he went away, wondering to himself what had happened.	*(skips here back to verse 3 for parallel)* 3 So Peter and the other disciple started for the tomb. 4 Both were running, but the other disciple outran Peter and reached the tomb first. 5 He bent over and looked in at the strips of linen lying there but did not go in. 6 Then Simon Peter, who was behind him, arrived and went into the tomb. He saw the strips of linen lying there, 7 as well as the burial cloth that had been around Jesus' head. The cloth was folded up by itself, separate from the linen. 8 Finally the other disciple,

			who had reached the tomb first, also went inside. He saw and believed. 9 (They still did not understand from Scripture that Jesus had to rise from the dead.) 10 Then the disciples went back to their homes,
		Jesus' appearance on the road to Emmaus (Luke 24:13-35)	
		36 While they were still talking about this, Jesus himself stood among them and said to them, "Peace be with you." 37 They were startled and frightened, thinking they saw a ghost. 38 He said to them, "Why are you troubled, and why do doubts rise in your minds? 39 Look at my hands and my feet. It is I myself! Touch me and see; a ghost	19 On the evening of that first day of the week, when the disciples were together, with the doors locked for fear of the Jews, Jesus came and stood among them and said, "Peace be with you!" 20 After he said this, he showed them his hands and side. The disciples were overjoyed when they saw the Lord. 21 Again Jesus said, "Peace be

		does not have flesh and bones, as you see I have."	with you! As the Father has sent me, I am sending you."
		[40] When he had said this, he showed them his hands and feet. [41] And while they still did not believe it because of joy and amazement, he asked them, "Do you have anything here to eat?" [42] They gave him a piece of broiled fish, [43] and he took it and ate it in their presence. [44] He said to them, "This is what I told you while I was still with you: Everything must be fulfilled that is written about me in the Law of Moses, the Prophets and the Psalms."	[22] And with that he breathed on them and said, "Receive the Holy Spirit. [23] If you forgive anyone his sins, they are forgiven; if you do not forgive them, they are not forgiven."
			[24] Now Thomas (called Didymus), one of the Twelve, was not with the disciples when Jesus came. [25] So the other

			disciples told him, We have seen the Lord!
			But he said to them, "Unless I see the nail marks in his hands and put my finger where the nails were, and put my hand into his side, I will not believe it."
			26 A week later his disciples were in the house again, and Thomas was with them. Though the doors were locked, Jesus came and stood among them and said, Peace be with you! 27 Then he said to Thomas, "Put your finger here; see my hands. Reach out your hand and put it into my side. Stop doubting and believe."
			29 Then Jesus told him, "Because you have seen me, you have believed; blessed are those who have not seen and

			yet have believed."

Appendix 2. A Possible Harmonization of the Resurrection Accounts

My esteemed Biblical exegesis professor at Fuller Theological Seminary, George Eldon Ladd, didn't really recommend a harmonization approach to the resurrection accounts. However, to answer his own question of whether the accounts *could* be harmonized, he worked out the following harmonization, he said, for my own amusement.[1] Later he found a nearly identical harmonization by Michael C. Perry. Here is George Ladd's approach to a harmonization:

1. The earthquake and removal of stone occurs before dawn.

2. A group of four women come early to the tomb, wondering who will move the stone. As they approach, they are amazed to see that the stone has been rolled away.

3. Mary rushes off to tell Peter and John that the body of Jesus has been stolen (John 20:2).

4. The other women stay in the garden. They enter the tomb and are met by two angels, who tell them to carry the word of the resurrection to the disciples.[3]

5. The women rush away from the garden, filled with mingled emotions of fear and joy, speaking to no one about the vision of the angels at the empty tomb (Mark 16:8).

6. Later in the day, Jesus met them. (Matthew 28:9 does not say that this meeting occurred in the garden.) They had to run away from the tomb. Jesus tells them to bear the word

---

[1] George Eldon Ladd, *I Believe in the Resurrection* (Eerdmans, 1975), pp. 91-93.

[2] Michael C. Perry, *The Easter Enigma* (London: Faber and Faber, 1959), pp. 65, 70.

[3] Ladd says, "The problem of a young man of Mark 16:5, two men of Luke 24:4, angels of Luke 24:23, is one of the ordinary Synoptic divergencies – of detail" (p. 92).

to the disciples; they depart to find the disciples, who are not together but scattered (Matthew 26:56).

7. Peter and John, having been informed by Mary, come to the tomb after the women have left. They see the clothes; vague comprehension dawns on John. they rush off to gather the disciples.

8. Mary returns to the tomb after Peter and John have left; they had run to the tomb (John 20:4), leaving Mary behind. She still thinks the body has been stolen. She is weeping outside the tomb, knowing nothing of the experience of the women she had left in the garden. She sees the two angels, then Jesus (John 20:11-17).[4]

9. After the first shock of amazement had worn off, the women find some of the disciples; the disciples cannot believe the fanciful story (Luke 24:11).

10. The disciples have gathered together.

11. Mary arrives and tells her experience (John 20:18).

12. That afternoon, the walk to Emmaus.

13. Sometime that afternoon, an appearance to Peter (Luke 24:34).

14. That evening, the disciples are all together in the closed room. They had been scattered, but the testimony of the women, of Peter and John, then of Mary, serves to bring them all together. Thomas was absent.

15. A second appearance to the eleven, including Thomas.

16. Galilee (Matthew 28:16). The appearance by Tiberias (John 21) and to the 500 brethren (1 Corinthians 15:6).

17. Return to Jerusalem; the final appearance and ascension.

Ladd concludes,

---

[4] Ladd notes that Mark's longer ending, 16:9 here, is not authentic (p. 92).

"This harmonization does not mean that the author intends to suggest that the events actually happened in this order. We cannot know."[5]

[5] Ladd, p. 93.

Appendix 3. Resurrection and Easter Hymns and Songs

Since Christ's resurrection is central to the Christian faith, mention of his resurrection occurs in literally thousands of songs and hymns. However, in the ones below the theme of resurrection is more strongly developed. Lyrics and tunes to the older hymns can usually be found in the CyberHymnal (www.cyberhymnal.org). Lyrics and tunes to the newer hymns and choruses can often be found in the Song Select feature of www.CCLI.com.

"All Ye that Seek the Lord Who Died," words: Charles Wesley (1746), music: Wenzel Müller. A 12-verse ballad of the resurrection story.

"Alleluia! Sing to Jesus," words: William C. Dix (1866), music: Rowland H. Prichard (1830)

"Because He Lives," words and music by William J. and Gloria Gaither (© 1971, William J. Gaither, Inc.; Gaither Copyright Management)

"Christ Arose!" words and music: Robert Lowry (1874)

"Christ Is Risen! Shout Hosanna!" words: Brian Wren (1984, © 1986 Hope Publishing Company), music: Polish carol, arranged by Edith M.G. Reed (1926), harmonized by Austin C. Lovelace (1964, © 1964, The United Methodist Publishing House)

"Christ Is Risen, Christ Is Risen," words: Archer T. Gurney (1862), music: Arthur S. Sullivan (1874)

"Christ the Lord Is Risen Today," words: Charles Wesley (1739), music: from *Lyra Davidica* (1708).

"Come, Ye Faithful, Raise the Strain," words: John of Damascus (8th century), translated by John M. Neale, music: Arthur S. Sullivan

"Crown Him with Many Crowns," words: Matthew Bridges (1851) and Godfrey Thring (1874), music: George J. Elvey (1868)

"Day of Resurrection, The," words: John of Damascus (8th century, *Anastaseōs hēmera*), translated by John M. Neale (1862); music Henry Smart (tune: Lancashire, 1835).

"Easter Song," by Anne Herring and Jack Schrader (©1974, Latter Rain Music, admin. by EMI Christian Music Publishing)

"He Arose" ("I believe in the resurrection of God's Son"), by Rick Muchow (© 1992, Rick Muchow, Encouraging Music).

"He Lives!" words and music: Alfred H. Ackley (© 1933, 1961, Rodeheaver Co., a div. of Word, Inc.)

"I Know That My Redeemer Lives," words: Charles Wesley, music: George F. Handel

"I Know that My Redeemer Lives," words: Samuel Medley (1775), music: Duke Street, attributed to John Hatton (1793)

"I Know That My Redeemer Liveth," words: Jessie Brown Pounds (1893), music: James H. Fillmore (1893)

"In the Tomb So Cold" ("Christ Is Risen"), by Graham Kendrick (© 1986, Thankyou Music, admin. by EMI Christian Music Publishing).

"Jesus Is Alive," by Ron Kenoly (© 1987, Integrity's Hosanna! Music).

"Lift Up, Lift Up Your Voices Now," words: John M. Neale (1851), music: John B. Calkin (tune: Waltham, 1872)

"O Sons and Daughters, Sing Your Praise," words: Jean Tisserand (15th century), translated by Ruth Duck (© 1993); music: 15th century French carol

"Strife Is O'er, the Battle Done," The, Latin (12th century, *Finita jam sunt praelia*), translated by Francis Pott (1861), music: Giovanni P. da Palestrina (1591), adapted by William Henry Monk (1861)

"Thine Is the Glory," words: Edmond L. Budry (1904), translated by R. Birch Hoyle (1923), music: George F. Handel (1746)

"Welcome, Happy Morning! Age to Age Shall Say," words: Venantius Fortunatus (c. 590, *Salve, festa dies*), translated by John Ellerton (1868), music: Arthur S. Sullivan (1872)

"You're Alive," by Graham Kendrick (© 1983, Thankyou Music, admin. by EMI Christian Music Publishing)

Appendix 4. Participant Notes for Classes and Groups

If you're working with a class or small group, feel free to duplicate the following handouts in this appendix at no additional charge. If you'd like to print 8-1/2" x 11" sheets, you can download the free Participant Guide handout sheets at: http://www.jesuswalk.com/resurrection/resurrection-lesson-handouts.pdf

Discussion Questions

You'll find several questions for each lesson. Each question may include several sub-questions. These are designed to get group members engaged in discussion of the key points of the passage. If you're running short of time, feel free to skip questions or portions of questions.

The notes include an outline and condensation of the lessons – particularly the scripture references – plus the discussion questions.

1. The Promise of Resurrection from the Dead
2. The Gospel Accounts of Christ's Resurrection from the Dead
3. Convincing Proofs of Christ's Bodily Resurrection
4. The Present-Day Significance of Christ's Resurrection
5. The Christian Hope of Resurrection at the Last Day

1. The Promise of Resurrection from the Dead

Resurrection Defined

Resurrection: Something more than a resuscitation after near death. Rather a raising up of the body after a period of being dead.

Old Testament Beginnings

Gathered to his fathers (Genesis 25:8)

Hebrew word *sheôl*, "the place of the dead," both good and bad. Seems to refer to the dark, deep regions, the land of forgetfulness ... a place of gloom and despair, a place where one can no longer enjoy life, and where the presence of Yahweh himself is withdrawn.

Psalm 6:5
Psalm 88:10-12

A Growing Hope of Resurrection

Progressive revelation.

Job 14:14
Job 19:25-27

Q1. How does Jobs vision of resurrection (Job 19:25-27) differ from the Jews former understanding of death as Sheol? What is progressive revelation?

Psalm 16:9-11
Hosea 13:14
Hosea 6:1-2
Isaiah 26:19
Isaiah 53:11

The phrase "light of life" (NIV) doesn't occur in the Masoretic Hebrew text, but is found in both the Greek Septuagint translation as well as the Hebrew text of the Isaiah scrolls found among the Dead Sea Scrolls.

Ezekiel 37:1-6

Daniel 12:1b-2

First Century Judaism

There were essentially three beliefs about the resurrection in Jesus' world.

1. Sadducees. Acts 5:17; Matthew 22:23; Acts 23:8

2. Pharisees

3. The Greeks and Romans (Acts 17:18, 32)

Jesus' Teaching on the Resurrection of the Dead

John 5:28-29

Acts 24:15

Luke 14:14

Q2. (John 5:28-29; Acts 24:15) According to scripture, both the righteous and unrighteous will experience resurrection. What will be the result of resurrection for the righteous?

Luke 20:34-36

Luke 20:37-38

Jesus' as the Agent of Resurrection

John 11:23-25

John 5:25, 28-29

John 6:39-40, 54

Q3. (John 11:23-25) What do you think Jesus meant when he said, I am the resurrection and the life? What role will Jesus play in the resurrection of the dead?

Jesus' Promise of His Own Resurrection

Matthew 16:21

Matthew 17:22-23

Matthew 20:17-19

The Third Day, Three Days

John 2:18-22; remembered by his enemies. Matthew 27:40; Mark 14:58

Matthew 12:39-40

Matthew 27:62-64

Q4. Why did Jesus' enemies heed his prediction of being raised on the third day even more than his disciples? Did his enemies expect him to rise? Did his followers?

2. The Gospel Accounts of Christ's Resurrection from the Dead

Before beginning, read the Resurrection accounts in the Gospels. Try looking at them as for the first time. Ask yourself: What happened here that prompted these stories? Look for differences as well as similarities.

Matthew 28:1-10, Mark 16:1-14, Luke 24:1-44, John 20:1-29

If you like, print out an online version that shows the Gospel resurrection accounts in parallel (NIV).
www.jesuswalk.com/resurrection/resurrection-parallels.htm

The Synoptic Problem

Synoptic Gospels – Matthew, Mark, Luke
Q, which stands for the German word *Quelle*, meaning source.
Mark – earliest gospel, Mark 16:9-19, the so-called longer ending of Mark
Matthew – Palestinian Jews
Luke – Hellenistic audience
John – eyewitness

Resurrection Differences

1. *Women.* In the Synoptic Gospels, Mary Magdalene and other women go to the tomb. In Johns account, Mary Magdalene goes alone.

2. *Appearance to the women.* In Matthew 28:9, Jesus appears to the women before they tell the disciples. In John 20:13-17, Jesus appears to Mary Magdalene first (also in the longer ending of Mark) – after she reports to the disciples. In Mark, the women tell no one of what they had seen.

3. *Number of angels.* In Matthew and Mark one angel appears; in Luke and John there are two angels.

4. *Purpose of the women's visit.* In Matthew they go to look at the tomb. In Mark and Luke they bring spices to anoint Je-

sus' body. In John, the anointing took place on Friday night and no purpose for Mary's visit is given.

5. *Grave clothes.* In Matthew and Mark, Jesus is wrapped in a large linen shroud (*sidrōn*). In John 19:40; 20:5-7 and Luke 24:12, Jesus is wrapped in strips of linen (*othonion*). See the discussion below.

6. *Location.* In Matthew and Mark, Jesus' resurrection appearances are in Galilee, while Luke only records appearances in the vicinity of Jerusalem.

Eyewitness Accounts

Q1. What differences do you find between the various resurrection accounts? How do you account for differences in eyewitness testimony? How might these differences add to the credibility of the witnesses?

Points of Agreement

1. Jesus was dead and buried.

2. The disciples were not prepared for Jesus' death. They were overcome with confusion.

3. The tomb was found on Easter morning to be empty. But this in itself didn't inspire faith. Mary thought the body was stolen.

4. The disciples encountered certain experiences which they took to be appearances of Jesus risen from the dead.

5. Contemporary Judaism had no concept of a dying and rising Messiah.

6. The disciples proclaimed the resurrection of Jesus in Jerusalem, near where he had been buried

What Happened Easter Morning?

1. Mary Magdalene saw him first and spoke to him (Mark 16:9, longer ending; John 20:16)

2. Other women also saw him and touched him (Matthew 28:9).

3. Jesus appeared to Peter and the other apostles (Luke 24:34; 1 Corinthians 15:5; Mark 16:14 longer ending; Luke 24:36).

4. Jesus appeared to Thomas (John 20:26-28).

5. Later, Jesus appeared to more than 500 at one time (1 Corinthians 15:6).

1 Corinthians 15:3-8

Q2. What similarities do you find in the resurrection accounts? Based on the agreements between the accounts, what seems to have happened?

The Grave Clothes

When you compare Luke 23:53 (*sindōn*) with Luke 24:12 (*othonion*) it appears that Luke, at least, is using the terms synonymously.

Luke 24:12, John 20:6-8

Q3. (Luke 24:12; John 20:6-8) What about the grave clothes brought Peter and John to faith? What was so peculiar about them?

What Was Jesus' Body Like?

1. Jesus described it as flesh and bones (Luke 24:39c).

2. He could eat (Luke 24:42-43; Acts 1:4)

3. His body could be touched and handled by others (Matthew 28:9; Luke 24:39b)

4. He could walk and talk (Luke 24:15), even cook (John 21:9), just as a normal human body.

5. Yet Jesus' wounds were still visible in his renewed body (Luke 24:39-40; John 20:20, 25-27)

6. Jesus could enter locked doors (John 20:19, 26) disappear (Luke 24:31) and appear (Luke 24:36) at will.

Q4. What do we know from the Gospels about the properties of Jesus' resurrection body? What was he capable of in this new body?

The Resurrection vs. the Ascension

Jesus' resurrection was when his body left the tomb and appeared alive to his disciples and others, never to die again.

Jesus' ascension occurred about 40 days after his resurrection and took place just outside of Jerusalem near Bethany:

Q5. What is the difference between Jesus' resurrection and his ascension? How do the two fit together? In what sense is the ascension the completion of the resurrection?

3. Convincing Evidence of Christ's Bodily Resurrection

Book blurb for *The Resurrection of Jesus* (1995) by Gerd Lüdemann:

> "What actually happened at the resurrection of Jesus? Using historical criticism and depth psychology, Lüdemann reviews the accounts of witnesses, consults Pauline texts, and investigates Easter events, concluding that though the quickening of Christ cannot be believed in a literal and scientific sense, we can still be Christians."

People Just Don't Come Back to Life

Western scientific worldview
Experience from the beginning of civilization

Historically Accessible

- Unrepeatable. It is a one-of-a-kind event that can't be studied

- Incomparable. We have no analogies to which to compare it

- Lacks credible evidence. This isn't actually true, but these scholars often explain away or neglect the strong evidence that we do have

A Narrow View of Historicity

N.T. Wright says the idea of history can be used in five different ways:

1. History as an event. Something that happened, whether we can prove it or not.

2. History as significant event. An historic event is one which carries momentous consequences.

3. History as a provable event. X may have happened, but since we can't prove it, therefore it isn't really historical.

4. History as writing about events in the past. It is historical in sense that it was written about – or talked about, as in oral history.

5. History as what modern historians can say about a topic, that which can be demonstrated and written within the post-Enlightenment world view. This is what liberal scholars mean when they reject the historical Jesus.

Alternate Theories of the Resurrection

Q1. What do you think motivates liberal Christian scholars to explain away the bodily resurrection of Jesus Christ? Why would they claim that it is unhistorical more than some other event in the first century?

1. Theft Theory

Matthew 28:11-15.
Motive, soldiers penalty of execution for sleeping, disciples face martyrdom for a lie

Q2. On the theft theory, what motive might the disciples have to take Jesus' body? What motive might the Romans have? The Jews? Joseph of Arimathea?

2. Swoon Theory

Heinrich Paulus (1828). Hugh J. Schonfield, *The Passover Plot* (1965).

3. Wrong Tomb Theory

Kirsopp Lake, *Historical Evidence for the Resurrection of Jesus Christ* (1907)

Matthew 27:61; Mark 15:47

4. Vision Theory

Rudolf Bultmann (1884-1976), demythologize the gospel to make it believable to modern man. He wrote in 1941 of the incredibility of a mythical event like the resuscitation of a corpse – for that is what resurrection means. The historian can perhaps to some extent account for that faith [in the resurrection] from the personal intimacy which the disciples had enjoyed with Jesus during his earthly life and so reduce the resurrection appearances to a series of subjective visions.

To refute this, Jesus' enemies could produce the body.
Also known as the Personality Influence Theory or Hallucination Theory
Inconsistent with the disciples' mental state. Doesn't explain Jesus' appearance to 500 persons at once.

5. Spiritual Metaphor Theory

Early Christians used terms such as dying and rising as a kind of metaphor to communicate their faith. When they said, Jesus was raised from the dead, so this view goes, they meant something like, He is alive in a spiritual, non-bodily sense, and we give him our allegiance as our lord. Only later did the church begin to take such expressions literally, according to this theory, and then penned the gospel accounts as a kind of secondary reinforcement of this belief.

Five Important Facts of Easter Morning

1. The Empty Tomb

2. The Undisturbed Grave Clothes

3. The Disciples' Psychological State

- That they weren't inclined to concoct a story of Jesus' resurrection.
- They weren't inclined to mistake Jesus' missing body for resurrection.
- They didn't expect any resurrection
- They weren't inclined to steal Jesus' body.

Q3. How does the disciples' psychological state after the crucifixion provide excellent support for belief in the resurrection?

4. The Post-Resurrection Appearances of Jesus

1. 1 Corinthians 15:3-8 was written 53-55 AD.

2. Mary Magdalene (John 20:14-17; Matthew 28:9-10; Mark 16:9)

3. The other Mary (Matthew 28:9-10)

4. Peter (Luke 24:34; 1 Corinthians 15:5)

5. Cleopas and another disciple on the road to Emmaus Sunday afternoon (Luke 24:13-35; Mark 16:12)

6. Disciples in Jerusalem Sunday evening (Luke 24:36-43; Acts 1:4; John 20:19-23; Mark 16:14; 1 Corinthians 15:5)

7. Thomas and the other disciples, a week later (John 20:24-29)

8. Disciples in Galilee (Matthew 28:17)

9. Disciples (Peter, Thomas, Nathanael, James, John, and two others) while fishing on the Sea of Galilee (John 21:1-23)

10. 500 at one time (1 Corinthians 15:6)

11. James, Jesus' brother, who later became the leader of the Jerusalem congregation (1 Corinthians 15:7)P14 P

12. Disciples at the ascension (Matthew 28:51-52)

13. Paul (1 Corinthians 15:8), much later

5. The Spread of Christianity

Declaring the resurrection in Jerusalem: Acts 2:24, 32; 3:15; 4:10, 33; 5:30

Growth of church in Jerusalem: Acts 2:41; 4:4; 6:7

Declaring the resurrection elsewhere: Acts 10:39-40; 13:29-30; 17:3, 31; 26:23

Arguments from Silence

- Lack of Biblical quotations
- Lack of Christ appearing first to male disciples
- Lack of emphasis on personal hope

- Lack of a portrait of Jesus

The Sufficiency of the Evidence

Q4. Which of the various proofs for the resurrection seems the most compelling to you? Why? If you had a friend who wasn't sure about the resurrection, could you explain why you're sure that Jesus was raised from the dead?

4. The Present-Day Significance of Christ's Resurrection

1. Jesus' Resurrection Is God's Seal of Approval on Jesus

Acts 2:32, 36; 5:30-31; 17:31; Romans 1:4

Q1. What kind of credibility would Jesus' ministry have had if he was not raised from the dead, especially when he predicted it ahead of time? In what way is the resurrection God's seal of approval on him?

2. Jesus' Resurrection Validates our Salvation

Romans 4:25; 1 Corinthians 15:13-19
Basis of our confidence: Romans 8:33-34; 1 Peter 1:21; Hebrews 4:14, 16

Q2. In what way does Christ's resurrection somehow validate that we are saved and forgiven by God? If we didn't believe Christ had been actually raised from the dead, how might we have doubts about our salvation?

3. Jesus' Resurrection Typifies our Spiritual Union with Him

Christ	Death and burial	Resurrection
Baptism	Immersed in the water	Brought out of the water
Believers	United with him in his death	Shall be united with him (in the future) in his resurrection

Romans 6:3-5; Colossians 2:12. 1 Peter 1:3; Romans 6:6, 8, 11; Galatians 5:20; Colossians 3:1-4; Ephesians 1:19b-20; 2:1, 4b-6

Q3. How does Christ's death and resurrection provide an analogy for baptism according to Romans 6:3-5 and Colossians 2:12? According to Ephesians 2:4-6, while being raised with Christ is still spiritual, not physical, in what way does this union impart real spiritual power?

4. Jesus' Resurrection Is the Harbinger of our Resurrection on the Last Day

1 Corinthians 6:14; 2 Corinthians 4:14; 1 Corinthians 15:20; Revelation 1:18)

Q4. What assurance do you have that you will be physically resurrected rather than experience disembodied immortality? What does it mean that Jesus is the firstfruits (1 Corinthians 15:20) and firstborn (Revelation 1:5) of the dead?

Q5. (1 Corinthians 15:58) What does being steadfast and immovable have to do with the hope of the resurrection? Why is our labor not in vain in the Lord?

5. The Christian Hope of Resurrection at the Last Day

Read again 1 Corinthians 15 and 1 Thessalonians 4:13-18.

Rapture vs. Resurrection

Rapture from the Latin noun *raptus*, which means, a carrying off (1 Thessalonians 4:17)

The order of events:

1. The **appearance** of Christ in the heavens,
2. The **angels trumpet** call summoning all God's people,
3. **Gathering** of his people, dead and alive (the quick and the dead) (Matthew 13:24-30, 37-43, 47-50; 25:31-46; 2 Thessalonians 2:1)
   a. **Resurrection** of those who are dead and
   b. **Changing** into resurrection bodies of those alive at that time.
4. Appearing before God's **judgment** (Revelation 20:11-13)
5. Entering into **glory**

Study Matthew 24:30-31; 1 Corinthians 15:51-52; 1 Thessalonians 4:16-17; Revelation 20:11-13
See also Romans 14:10; 2 Corinthians 5:10

Q1. What is the word used in the Bible instead of rapture? When will the resurrection take place in relation to Christ's return? In relation to judgment? In relation to glory? (This is *not* the place to debate various theories of the rapture and the millennium. Be kind and loving!)

In Heaven Prior to the Resurrection

In 1 Thessalonians 4:14; Philippians 1:23-24; 2 Corinthians 5:8; Revelation 6:9-11; 7:9, 14; John 14:2-3

Q2. (Philippians 1:23-24; 2 Corinthians 5:8) According to these verses, where will Christians be immediately after death? Where do we await the resurrection?

Redemption and Glorification

Redemption. Romans 8:23-24a

Glorification. *Believers resurrection*: 1 Corinthians 15:43; also Romans 8:17, 30; 2 Corinthians 3:18; 4:17; Philippians 3:21; Colossians 1:27; 3:4; 2 Thessalonians 2:14; 2 Timothy 2:10; Hebrews 2:10

Jesus' resurrection: Luke 24:26; John 7:39; 12:16, 23; 13:31; Acts 3:13; Colossians 3:4; 1 Timothy 3:16; Hebrews 2:9; 1 Peter 1:11, 21

Corruptible vs. Incorruptible, Natural vs. Spiritual Bodies

1 Corinthians 15:35, 42-44

- Corruptible - Incorruptible
- Dishonor - Glory. Glory, *doxa*, "the condition of being bright or shining, brightness, splendor, radiance."
- Weakness - Power
- Natural - Spiritual

Q3. What does the phrase redemption of our bodies(Romans 8:23-24) tell us about our resurrection? What words in 1 Corinthians 15:42-44 describe our resurrection bodies?

What Is Our Resurrection Body Going to Be Like?

1 John 3:2; Philippians 3:21; 1 Corinthians 15:49

Incorruptible (1 Corinthians 15:42), glorified (1 Corinthians 15:43a), powerful (1 Corinthians 15:43b), able to navigate in the spiritual realm (1 Corinthians 15:44).

Luke 20:34-36

Why Will We Have Resurrection Bodies?

2 Peter 3:12-13; Revelation 21:1, 5; Revelation 5:10

Q4. What will our resurrection bodies be like? Why do you think we will be given resurrection bodies? What is the point?

Getting All the Right Molecules Restored

Death Is Not the Victor

1 Corinthians 15:26; 2 Peter 3:13; Revelation 21:1, 5; Isaiah 65:17-19; 66:22; 1 Corinthians 15:51-53, 57

Q5. Why should Christians look forward to the events surrounding our resurrection? Why do you think Christians have largely lost this as their active expectation and hope? What should be done to reclaim these truths?